I will And be
Every Day
day.

YOU DON'T HAVE TO BE BORN BRILLIANT YOU ARE!

coincidences:
Bought this book.
trying to find some music
on cassette — found music n channel
& words were You are
beautiful on the inside.
Keep reaching for your highest
aspirations

Moving into a New Phase of my life.

Getting to know Chris. who is Positive.

Shawn & Gerri & Andy leaving my life. who are negative.

Making Room for New Friends

Thankyou Universe.

YOU DON'T HAVE TO BE BORN BRILLIANT

How to Design a Magnificent Life

John McGrath

HODDER

A Hodder Book

Published in Australia and New Zealand in 2000
by Hodder Headline Australia Pty Limited
(A member of the Hodder Headline Group)
Level 22, 201 Kent Street, Sydney NSW 2000
Website: www.hha.com.au

Copyright © John McGrath 2000

This book is copyright. Apart from any fair dealing for
the purposes of private study, research, criticism or
review permitted under the *Copyright Act 1968*,
no part may be stored or reproduced by any process
without prior written permission. Enquiries should
be made to the publisher.

**National Library of Australia
Cataloguing-in-Publication data**

McGrath, John, 1963- .
 You don't have to be born brilliant : how to design a
 magnificent life.

 ISBN 0 7336 0796 9.

 1. Success. 2. Success - Psychological aspects. 1. Title.

158.1

Produced by Brewster Publishers Pty Ltd
Cover design by Nick Morgan, Moon Design
Text design and typesetting by Bookhouse, Sydney
Printed in Australia by Griffin Press, Adelaide

I dedicate this book to my family, friends and team. I am blessed to be surrounded by some of the most inspiring and decent people on the planet for which I am eternally grateful. In particular the 'Red Elvis'; Luc; Siimon; Will; Grant and Lisa; Paul and Karen; Maddie; Matt and Jodie; Michael; Scruffy; JD; and of course my mum. Thank you, you have all been life-long friends who supported and inspired me during the tough times. I look forward to our future journey together.

CONTENTS

Before you start   ix

PART 1: LAYING THE FOUNDATIONS

Success leaves clues	3
The lotto approach to life	12
Black belt of the mind	23

PART 2: CREATING A LIFE PLAN

Sliding doors	45
Look after the big rocks first	65
First we make our habits then our habits make us	95
Blockages in the arteries of success	97
24 hours	115

PART 3: STAYING SUCCESSFUL

Inspiration is all around us	133
Conducting a personal audit	138
Perfect health	151
Nice guys and girls *don't* finish last	170
The habit of making money	185
Some final tips for success and growth	205

Before you go   208

Before you start

Thank you for choosing this book—I know there are many of its kind to choose from. The fact that you have picked it up off the shelf in the bookshop means that you have the interest and initiative to make a difference to your life. Or, if you've been given the book, it means there is someone positive in your life who wants to encourage and guide you along to the next level. Either way, things are about to go very right for you.

Chances are there aren't too many things in your life that you will need to change in order to achieve whatever it is you desire. It's simply a matter of deciding what your goals are and developing a plan to achieve them. I look forward to helping you do that.

This book has been a long time coming. I actually sat down to write it five years ago but, despite the many lessons I had already learned, I was impeded by the same elements I will discuss in this book: fear, procrastination and uncertainty. I mention this because I don't want you to think that fear and uncertainty will necessarily ever disappear from your life; you just get better at handling them and learn to see them in a different way. The fact we are now talking means that I conquered those fears and the book is finished. I hope you enjoy it.

You Don't Have to be Born Brilliant is a book about life—specifically, about designing a magnificent life, whatever that may mean to you. If you have some sense that you could improve the quality of your life in any area—relationships, health, finance or business—this book can be the catalyst to make it happen.

Success in life is too rare a commodity. For many years I've been disappointed and frustrated to observe how so few people actually achieve their life goals in this magnificent world. Amazingly, only about

2% of the population manage to achieve their major life goals and, more importantly, get to enjoy the incredible journey of self-discovery and personal development that accompanies these achievements.

Many people suffer from the misconception that if they just 'hang in there' and wait long enough, success may come their way. They drift around wondering where the keys to success may be hidden. The fact is, the keys are hanging on their belt. They only have to learn which keys are useful and start to use them.

Unfortunately, most people have been trained or programmed to think conservatively—to think small, if you like. They are taught not to aim too high in case they get disappointed. I call this small poppy training. What most people don't realise is that you can reprogram your thought patterns, attitudes and beliefs, no matter what they may be at present, to whatever you would like them to be. And you can do it in an instant.

Think about it. Many people would admit that they have a tendency to be somewhat negative in life, often being overly critical, cynical or unsupportive. And there is no one who couldn't argue that being negative in your thought processes is one of the greatest barriers to success and happiness. So why not change to being positive?

I believe we can all have everything we desire if we have total clarity about what it is we want, create a plan to steer us on the journey, and passionately experience every day of our life.

My observations come from personal experience. It was only a short time ago that my life was more a nightmare than a dream. I was broke, uninspired and going nowhere faster than anyone I knew. Then something happened to give me a sense of direction, and I subsequently found that with some minor adjustments life could turn 360 degrees in a matter of months. This book tells the story of how that happened and recounts the key lessons and observations I learned along the way.

Small poppy thinking is one of the diseases of our time. Many people have lost sight of their dreams—or even worse, lost hope. I hope this book can reignite your passion and turn up the flame to allow you to burn as brightly as every other star in the sky. And for those who are already achieving greatness, there are also useful messages within these pages about the dark side of success—diseases such as complacency, arrogance and greed—that can help you navigate a different set of challenges that come as you create more success within your life.

Whatever messages are within this book for you, I hope you'll find it an adventure, with every chapter a new area of discovery. I've written it so you can read it either from cover to cover or just dip into it when you need some support or inspiration.

And for those who are reading this book hoping that everything will be OK when you achieve success—when you get 'there'—I must let you know up front that there is no 'there'. One of the first secrets of success I learned is that it's the journey that must be the reward, not the destination. Every hour of every day is there for you to use, enjoy, grow in and cherish.

Before you begin there are two things I ask of you. Firstly, approach the book with an open mind and a sense of curiosity. If you read from a position of judgment, you won't take many new ideas on board. Secondly, act immediately on what you read. If you come across something that strikes a chord with you, put the book down and start on it right away. If you're asked to make a list of your goals, put the book down mid-page and write down your goals. Action creates momentum and momentum is critical.

So fasten your seatbelts: you're in for the ride of your life! See you at the end.

PART 1

Laying the Foundations

Success leaves clues

Why is it that two people in the same place at the same time and with the same opportunities often deliver incredibly different results? In business I consistently find that in most sales teams there's always one or two salespeople who dramatically outperform the others, despite the fact that they're selling the same product at the same time to the same market.

And why is it that some people seem to keep themselves physically fit with apparent ease while most people are struggling to reduce their weight or fight off illness?

Well, a good place to find the answer is to study

those who are achieving the results that inspire you: find out what they do differently to the rest. This was the starting point for me. I'll take you back to 1982, when my life was out of control.

It was my dream to become a professional footballer. I had the ability. Although I wasn't good at much else at the time, I was a good footballer. As I wanted to become a professional rugby league player, I had seen very little point in studying hard at school. I'd spent nearly all my time at the gym or on the football field practising and very little in class or at the library. Consequently, my last two years at Sydney Boys High School provided very little in the way of academic success—a self-inflicted pain I had to endure. In fact, I ended up achieving one of the lowest marks imaginable in my leaving year.

So in 1982, when it came time to take my lousy mark and step into the real world, I had pinned all my hopes on a football career. Within 90 days of leaving school I suffered a collapsed lung after a Friday night representative game early in the season, and had to undergo extensive surgery, leaving me unable to play football again. So here I was with a poor academic record, unable to play football and staring at a long life of mediocrity. I couldn't have imagined a worse situation if I'd tried.

But this is where my first major life lesson was learned. (Since that time I've found that most of my most inspirational learning originated from painful experiences.) Within six months I was to have understood that what happens to you in life is inconsequential. What matters is your *response* to life's twists and turns.

I was to find out very quickly that things that can sometimes appear to be earthquakes in your life are incredible opportunities in disguise. I temporarily saw my poor exam results and injury as a setback, but in fact they were to become the foundations of my earliest successes.

I was depressed for the first few months following the operation. I couldn't bring myself to tell my family and friends the real result I had received. I had no money and very few job prospects, and I had to compete in a tight job market with people who had far better résumés than myself. It was from this depression that inspiration was born. I had hit the lowest point in my life when I heard a friend of mine say to someone that he read a great book called *Think and Grow Rich* by Napoleon Hill—a book that taught you how to achieve whatever you wanted.

I thought perhaps I should also read such a book, but having refused to read any of the mandatory literature at school the previous two years, I felt some initial discomfort and had reservations about going out to buy it. In addition to that, I could hardly afford it! But something within told me to take the step: buy the book. So I did, and that was the first of many subsequent events that allowed me to turn my life around.

For perhaps the first time ever, Napoleon Hill's words caused me to revisit my past actions and decisions and take responsibility for my life. I started to see the link between my thoughts, beliefs, decisions, actions and habits and the pathetic place I found myself in.

And with that new acceptance of responsibility came the understanding that if I had created this mess I could also clean it up. I could create something totally different for myself. And the ensuing years were to prove to me that it could happen in an incredibly short space of time.

So, armed with a new set of thoughts and a very different attitude to life, I started to review exactly what I wanted to achieve for myself. This was a little difficult at first as I had already gone part of the way down the road of accepting mediocrity as my benchmark.

I know a lot of teenagers feel as depressed and hopeless as I did then, and many accept it as their lot in life and don't do anything about it. In my own case there was another emotion: frustration. I came to feel terribly frustrated at how life was turning out, and it was this frustration that eventually jolted me into action. I made use of the dissatisfaction and depression I felt: I harnessed the energy and turned it around.

I recognised that I, and nobody else, was responsible for the position I found myself in. This acceptance was a huge step forward. Until then, I'd made the usual mistake of blaming other people. For example, I'd never accepted responsibility for scoring 95 out of 500 in my final school exams. Instead, I blamed my teachers, my parents and my upbringing. Now I saw clearly that the only person responsible for those lousy marks was me. As a corollary of this,

I also saw that the only person who could change it was me.

So I set about cleaning up my act and, in doing so, I felt uplifted. Each of the various changes I made to my life made me feel good and these good feelings, in turn, created confidence and gave me a new sense of enthusiasm and excitement. My self-esteem shot up. I also felt I was restoring myself in the eyes of my parents, which was very important to me at the time and was actually a major motivation. My father died a couple of years later and I now regret very much that he did not live to see me get ahead in life.

*

Think and Grow Rich was the first of many hundreds of books I have since read on the subject of success and achievement. Each and every book supported my belief that success leaves clues.

One thing I discovered about those who achieved success is that very few of them were successful to begin with. In fact, the vast majority of the '2% Club'—those living their dreams—were not from wealthy families. Nor had they necessarily enjoyed the benefits of a good education. Very few people, I discovered, ever left the maternity ward as entrepreneurs or successful salespeople. In almost every case, success was self-created.

Many people don't realise this. Their excuse for being part of the population who aren't successful is that the people who make up the other 2 per cent somehow had success thrust upon them by circumstances or pure luck, or were born with a super-abundance of talent or intelligence that ensured success came to them naturally. This, of course, is a myth.

As we all know, a high IQ and a university degree certainly don't guarantee success. This isn't to suggest, of course, that education doesn't matter and isn't a great starting point. For many people, education is the foundation of a successful career. So if you've got a high IQ and you're academically inclined, that's fantastic; you've got a great start in life. But if you hate studying and you've never passed an exam in your life, that's OK too. There are many commercial opportunities today for which the key requirement is not education but intuition, energy, integrity, common sense or a likeable personality—

so don't feel inadequate if your passage so far has not been traditional.

Look at the Australian actor Russell Crowe, undoubtedly one of the great talents of our time. He was a close school friend of mine back at Sydney Boys' High. Russell is the only person I know from school who got thrown out of the classroom more often than I did. We would have been voted by the teachers as the guys least likely to succeed. He didn't go on to do his HSC, which was a pity, because I'm sure it would have been a close contest between us for the wooden spoon in our year.

But Russell had a passion: it was, of course, acting. Even while we were at school he'd occasionally get parts as an extra on film sets, where his father used to work as a caterer. He made the most of the opportunity: he watched, listened and learned. He'd speak to actors and ask them how they developed their craft. Gradually, bit by bit, he learned the secrets of the trade.

I'm sure Russell's parents must have had some reservations when he told them he'd decided to become an actor. It's a tough profession where the large majority struggle to break in. Thankfully for moviegoers around the world, Russell took up the challenge and stared it in the face. The rest is history for the young lad from Sydney who now earns $25 million a movie. Today, he's on top of the world because he made his passion his career.

Learning: Successful people adopt certain approaches to life that can be learned and implemented by anyone. Study the system of success and develop a personal strategy for achievement. Do what you love with commitment and dedication and success is guaranteed.

The lotto approach to life

Why do such a select few achieve success? Is it a matter of luck? Is it being in the right place at the right time? Do some people just inherit the right genes? Success has very little to do with any of these things: essentially success is generated from a state of mind.

Success is a system that can be learned and applied like a mathematical formula. Even so, some people decide to adopt the lotto approach to life. Just as they might head down to their local newsagent each Monday, hoping to circle the right numbers, so they sit and watch life's lotto draw, ticket in hand, desperately praying that this is their week. The odds that it'll be them achieving the dream of winning lotto are about 1 in 50 million. On the other hand, the odds that you'll achieve your dreams if you follow the success principles in this book are about 97% guaranteed.

BE THE ARCHITECT OF YOUR LIFE

Success is a logical consequence of approaching life with a particular attitude. There is a system we can follow to achieve success, and it's a system anyone can learn. You don't have to be academically bright; you don't have to have done a course; it doesn't cost money. And it doesn't even take a long time. All you have to do initially is adopt the right attitude.

I've met dozens of highly successful people in my life and I can't think of one who hasn't had an incredibly positive attitude to life. We've already learnt that success leaves clues. Successful people are enthusiastic and optimistic; they know exactly where they're headed; they're not put off by failure because they believe every obstacle can be overcome; and they have the persistence and stamina to see things through to the end.

Can you turn yourself into someone like that? Of course you can. You might think that changing your attitude involves changing your personality, but it doesn't. Changing your personality would probably be impossible, anyway. Rest assured that you can be shy and have a positive attitude. You can be funny, intense, playful or serious and develop a great mindset. It doesn't matter what your personal style is: you can turbo-charge your attitude.

Many people believe that life's hurdles are largely outside their control: that they're born into the wrong family; that they have the wrong education; that they never get the right breaks in life. These are called limiting beliefs, and it's this kind of thinking that prevents or repels success. When you turn that around—when you start to believe that you have the capacity to take control you will find your life transformed.

So, how do you recognise what your limiting beliefs are? It's really quite easy. Complete this sentence with reference to an area in which you've been unable to create the results you desire for yourself: 'I'm not achieving this result in this area of my life because…' and whatever comes out of your mouth thereafter will be a limiting belief. Guaranteed.

Let's try it. Say you're struggling financially. 'I'm

not wealthy or financially secure because…'. I'll take a guess at what would likely be the end of that sentence for some people: 'Because my boss hasn't given me a pay rise for two years'. Or 'Because my family has never had money; we're not good at it'.

Here's a reality check. If you're not financially secure it's likely that you don't have a budget, you spend more money than you earn and you've created a downward spiral of debt around you. Enter the empowering belief that could go something like: 'I can create financial success quickly with the correct approach. A sensible budget will deliver me a financial surplus which, when invested in capital-appreciating assets and leveraged by the magic of compound growth, will create financial success for me.'

When you change your outlook in ways like this you'll realise that you have the power to be the architect of your own life. Adopting a positive set of beliefs will fundamentally change every area of your life.

OVERCOMING INERTIA

Taking action is the key. Transforming your attitudes and habits is like a Qantas 747 taking off. To get the plane moving along the tarmac requires great energy and effort, because there's a lot of inertia to overcome. Then getting it airborne also requires further thrust and power. Eventually, though, when the plane breaks through the clouds, it can cruise at high speed with far less effort.

The process of change outlined in this book follows the same pattern. It can be hard and sometimes painful to begin with, because you may have to overcome the pull of gravity that keeps you on the ground, wedged between the small poppies. But once you reach cruising speed and altitude, you'll find it becomes much easier. You will do what you need to do almost without thinking, carried along by your own momentum.

LOOKING ON THE BRIGHT SIDE OF THINGS

Like everyone I often react with the usual knee-jerk feeling of disappointment when something goes wrong. I think to myself, 'I can't believe that—how did I let that happen?' An instant later though, a default mechanism takes over in my mind, pushing out the sense of disappointment. I have done this for so long that it's now become automatic. I start to look at what has happened in a new way: 'Why did it happen? How can I prevent it from happening again? What can I learn from the experience? How can I turn it to my advantage?' Then I move on: 'NEXT!' This is critical when you encounter failure. Say to yourself, 'OK, it didn't work, it didn't happen, but I'm ready to move on to the next thing'.

Life has taught me many lessons. One important one, which I utilise consistently, is that to be successful you need to have a dozen balls in the air at one time, because inevitably five or six of them are going to fall to the ground. Everyone has to expect that kind of failure rate—it's logical that if you're always stretching yourself to new levels and challenging the status quo, not everything will go to plan. To be successful and have a great life you need only five or six balls to stay in the air. You don't need to have everything work out for you *all* the time. What you need is for a few key things to work out for you *some* of the time.

Some people put all their eggs in one basket: they embark on one major project, and if it doesn't work out as they had hoped they retreat into a hole. As an example on any day I might send out ten letters to people I would like to do business with, knowing that possibly only one will ever lead to anything. What's important is not that nine of those approaches I made came to nothing, but that one could lead to new business.

FAILURE AND SUCCESS ARE PART OF THE SAME PACKAGE

I'd like to say at this point that I'm far from proud of my abysmal results at school. I only told the story for those who have been challenged academically and have felt (incorrectly) that they'd have to take a back seat position in life while the straight A students drove the bus. I also mentioned Russell Crowe in the first chapter, now I'd like to introduce you to Kelli Fox—or Kelli Herd, as I knew her in school.

Kelli and I met when we were teenagers. We were great friends. She went to the girls school next to mine. Kelli came from a working-class family and used to live in a tiny two-bedroom weatherboard cottage with her mother and grandmother in a rough neighbourhood near our schools. She did not achieve tremendous results at school either—certainly nothing to suggest her future achievements. At 17 years of age Kelli left Sydney Girls High School and we lost contact. I later ran into someone who knew us both and recounted this wonderful story of Kelli's path since school.

Like Russell, Kelli had had a passion. In her case it was for astrology. After finishing school she had gone to a local Technical College to develop her interests and expertise in this area. Simultaneously she developed her skills in the area of computing, another area of interest for her.

It was in the computing world, while working for Apple computers, that she met David Fox. David was also a very passionate, focused and committed IT exponent and before too long these two had hit it off. Within two years they were married. After studying the market and considering their areas of expertise, they decided to combine Kelli's passion and interest in astrology with David's skills in computers and direct them towards a fast-growing new concept called the Internet. And as the Australian market was relatively short on Internet opportunity back then, they decided to move to America to see if their online astrology concept could work.

After spending several years developing and refining their website they reached a critical point—they were several weeks away from financial disaster. They had very little money when they first went to America but now the well was almost dry. So in desperation they sought a joint venture partner—someone who understood their vision, could support their growth, and just as importantly, would pay them a wage before it was too late! They approached several large Internet companies they felt were suitable, explained their concept, then went home and prayed.

One company called ivillage.com was about to float their company on the stock exchange and loved Kelli and David's site. After a round of discussions they agreed to sell their site to ivillage.com for a small amount of money and some shares in the upcoming float. For Kelli and David there was very little option, as time was running out for their finances. History now shows that the shares they owned in the ivillage.com float were valued at over $100 million just weeks after the float! Imagine, a young girl from a working-class background who placed the bet on herself; someone who ventured to the other side of the world and struck it rich as a result of her vision, hard work, planning and resilience.

I'd like to think that there's a bit of Kelli Fox in all of us—an ordinary person who achieved extraordinary results.

STAY FOCUSED

In life, failure alternates naturally with success. Don't worry if many of the things you try don't work out. If you attempt five new things this year—you move house, start a new exercise regimen, begin a new job, launch an investment program, try your arm at a new sporting activity—and if some of them don't work out, it really doesn't matter. The fact that two or three *did* work will mean you're much further advanced than you were at the beginning of the year.

So stay focused on what goes right—leave the non-desired outcomes by the side of the road. It's an interesting fact that most people can have 100 great things happening in their life at any one time and one problem—and where do you think their thoughts are centred? Invariably on the one thing not working. Fix it or forget it, then move on.

One cautionary word before you launch into your new life: I don't want you to be naive about a thing called lag time. Lag time is the space between when you start an action and when you receive the benefits. For example, if having decided you want a better body shape you check out the local gym and pay a casual visit for an hour, don't expect to look like Arnold Schwarzeneger that afternoon! That's naive. There will be a period of readjustment and *then* you'll see results—often small at first—but they *will* arrive. Guaranteed. If you persist.

Learning: Achieving success in life is *not* like entering the lottery—it is more like a predictable science. Some people wait for their number to be called hoping for success some day while others develop a plan, take action and create opportunity to build their own path to success, today. Be very clear that success is not achieved by 'smoke and mirrors'—it's done through clarity, planning and action.

Black belt of the mind

There are many similarities between learning a martial art and taking control of your mind. Both are a choice, a skill, and both are attainable by all of us. Given sufficient time and instruction, anyone can become a karate black belt. It's a matter of knowing where to start, being shown what it will take, practising the discipline and constantly improving. So it is with becoming a black belt of the mind. There are several skills to master and they fall into five categories: empowering beliefs; enthusiasm and passion; positive thinking; persistence; focusing on what you can control. We'll look at them one at a time.

EMPOWERING BELIEFS

Most of us were raised in small poppy environments. As a consequence, many of us have developed a set of belief structures that don't support excellence, happiness and success. Let me explain.

If you are female and were raised to believe that it's a man's world, full of glass ceilings for women, this belief system would be like driving around every day in a magnificent sports car with the handbrake on. You may not think consciously about the belief on a day-to-day basis, but if it's part of your make-up it'll hold you back whether you're aware of it or not—just like a handbrake will slow you down. Replace that particular belief with one that says, 'The world rewards high achievers who live their life with passion and integrity' (note that there's no mention of gender). Now, all of a sudden, the handbrake comes off and you start reaching your chosen destinations faster and with less effort.

An example of this was when I started selling real estate. I had wanted to start my own business while still young, and knew I needed to get into an industry that would allow me to do that. There seemed two possibilities that interested me: real estate and travel. Both were in the business of selling, both were people-oriented, and both were services I felt I could relate to.

I chose real estate. I tried for a job at several companies and finally landed one renting flats and houses. So, after a year at a car dealership, I was making a fresh start. I threw myself into the real estate job. I realised the first thing I needed to do was acquire in-depth product knowledge—knowledge about property, architecture, the market place, values. By studying books at the library I learned what was a Federation house, a Victorian house, an Edwardian house, and so on, and I learned it well enough to discuss the subject with customers.

I learned all about property values. I went to auctions almost every night, most of them run by other companies, and sat at the back with my clipboard, noting down the prices paid for each property. Next day I'd make a point of driving past each property and equating it mentally with the price paid for it. At the auctions I watched carefully what the good salespeople did: how they worked the room, how they related to customers. Often I'd position myself next to people who were bidding, so when the agent came to speak to them I could hear what was said. It was fun and I thrived on it. Going to work each day was like going to Disneyland.

With so much knowledge gained, and having worked in rentals for two years, I decided to move into sales. I was only 20 years old. In an industry that was typically dominated by more mature folk, being so young was a slight departure from the norm in the area of sales but I thought I could do it. I was committed, excited, prepared to work as hard as I could and determined that nothing would stop me. So off I went to follow my dream.

On the day I started I ran into a gentleman I knew. He had been in the industry a long while and though he hadn't achieved any great success he was nonetheless a skilled salesperson. I had developed respect for him—perhaps predominantly based upon his senior status. He asked what I was up to and I told him that I had decided to leave my position in property management and start selling. He looked at me somewhat strangely and shook his head with concern. 'You should have talked to me before you made the decision. You don't realise that people buying and selling real estate don't want to deal with someone your age. They want someone with more grey hair, someone they can confide in and relate to.'

Wow. I couldn't believe it! My energy and enthusiasm went from 10/10 to 4/10. All of a sudden I doubted my ability, believing that someone with his experience surely couldn't be wrong. And after trying to sell real estate for several months I realised that he was right: I was not getting anywhere. My belief patterns had been reprogrammed merely at this gentleman's suggestion. So here I was in a state of despair. I had left a solid job, where I had built up a small position of seniority, and 'erroneously' moved into a risky job that I was starting to sense I was unqualified for. I was now unsure if I was doing the right thing.

In the meantime I had written a letter to a gentleman in America who was hailed as the top real estate salesman in the world at the time, requesting the opportunity to meet with him. His name was Nicholas Barson. Mr Barson responded by saying that he'd be happy for me to visit him to see what he did. I figured I had nothing to lose. I decided to go to New York for three days to see if I could learn any of his secrets.

I had never been overseas in my life, so this was a big deal for me, especially knowing how poorly I had performed in the first few months of my new career. Irrespective of my anxieties, I jumped on a plane for the first time and travelled to the Big Apple. I was terrified at my first glimpse of the other side of the world, but it was an event that would change my life forever.

I met Mr Barson within two hours of arriving in New York. He was tall, well presented and wore a gold jacket. I was immediately impressed by how 'normal' he appeared (despite the gold jacket). Not a stereotypical, smooth sales type; just a regular guy. I asked him about real estate and why he had outperformed every other real estate salesperson on the planet. He talked with enthusiasm and optimism. He told me how he had come from a large, working-class migrant family and how real estate had been his opportunity to create a new life for himself. He was polite. Attentive. Passionate and busy. I told him that I had hoped to follow in his footsteps, to one day be the best real estate salesperson on the planet, too. He smiled and said to me, 'Why one day? Why not now?'

That comment stopped me in my tracks. No one had ever talked to me like that before. It felt a little uncomfortable at first, but it started me thinking. I told him that my first few months had been anything but successful; in fact, I was on the verge of quitting. Then I told him that my learned friend in Sydney had suggested I was too young for sales and that my sales figures to date were certainly starting to confirm his theory.

He looked at me in amazement. He said, 'John, I was born poor. I have only learned to speak English in the last 15 years. I had no education. And yet none of these facts have had anything to do with my success or otherwise. If you're good enough, you're old enough!'

*

Beliefs are the foundation of our lives. If your beliefs are empowering they allow you to achieve almost anything—if they're limiting then almost everything will see like a massive challenge and invariably you'll find dead ends that'll reinforce your negative beliefs. Mind you, an empowering belief won't instantly ensure success but it does pave the way for the possibility of great outcomes.

Let's look at it. Two people working in the same showroom, selling the same product to the same market. A customer walks in and the salesperson with a limiting belief sees them as a distraction; a tyre kicker who'll probably end up wasting part of their day and will probably never buy anything from anyone. How do you think they'll treat the customer? Their body language and speech will send off messages that will repel them—and then the salesperson will walk back into the office and tell his colleagues 'I told you they were a waste of time'.

Enter the other salesperson who sees them as an important person whether they buy anything or not. She believes that if they are well looked after, listened to and acted upon they're likely to buy something or at least refer someone else to her who will buy something. She sees them as an opportunity to provide excellent service and add value through her knowledge and sales skills. The relationship in this instance is highly likely to go in a very different direction—one that will lead to fulfilment and business—and more than likely a life long business relationship or source of referral.

The way you look at life has an enormous impact

on your results. Scrutinise your beliefs and reject any that aren't likely to support your goals and improve the quality of your life and those around you.

ENTHUSIASM AND PASSION

The exact moment that Nicholas Barson said those words to me I felt my life change. A tingle ran down my spine, and still does today, when I recall that moment. I was no more qualified for success the moment after that advice than I was the moment before, but the difference was that I had a new belief structure about success and what created it. Mr Barson had gone on to say, 'Do you really think customers want great advice, an enthusiastic person to work with, sound product knowledge, someone who cares—or do you think they crave grey hair?' The answer was obvious. I returned home a different person than I had left, thanks entirely to Nicholas Barson.

Being successful is a learnable skill. It isn't a talent we're born with. We either work it out ourselves or we learn it from others. Learning from others can be vital to our own success. Sports people always do it. I'm sure all ambitious young golfers spend a lot of time studying the techniques of the great players to see what makes them so good and then, by trial and error, attempting to do it themselves. We should all do the same thing in whatever field we wish to be successful. Identify the people who have made it to the top and study how they operate, whether by watching them in action, reading about them or, better still, speaking to them personally.

I try to make sure that the people I spend time with are positive people whom I can learn from; people who can inspire me to greater heights. Surrounding oneself with positive people is also a type of insurance. When things go badly, as they do for all of us from time to time, the presence of positive people acts as a safety net. With positive people around you, you are better able to push onto and over the next hurdle.

*

By having a great attitude you will create a wonderful environment for yourself. A great attitude also acts like a magnet: if you have a great attitude you'll attract great and interesting people to you. If your energy—which is manifested in your attitude—is not at a high level you will not only fail to attract such people to you, you'll actually repel opportunities away from you.

Passion is a wonderful tool for success and a beautiful way to live your life. And the most exciting part about it is it's available to every single person on the planet in an instant. You don't need a degree, years of experience or even something great to happen—all you need is the desire to achieve your dreams then to get turned on by life.

I've often heard people say, 'If I had those things happen in my life I'd be passionate, too.' And I think to myself they've missed the point completely. The real truth is if only they'd get passionate they'd have all those things in their life!

So make the decision—start throwing everything into whatever you've got right now. Give of yourself 100% in your career, your family, your friendships—in fact everything that's important enough to be on your To Do list or calendar should be done with 100% passion and enthusiasm. You won't have to wait long until you see and feel the results.

POSITIVE THINKING

Most of us underestimate the power of thought. We assume we can think negative thoughts and live life in a positive manner. But whatever we practise in private will inevitably be revealed in public. So don't delude yourself into thinking that you can allow yourself ongoing negative thoughts and turn on a positive thought when the need arises. You must have your mind tuned to the most positive thoughts possible. I call it tuning in to Channel 37—the positive channel. I use the metaphor of a television channel because that's how easy it is to switch from one thought process to another. Just as you would switch from a program that you found boring or depressing with the click of a remote you can do the same with your attitude. Whether you call your positive state Channel 37 or Channel 22 is immaterial —what matters is that you recognise that your state of mind is changeable at any time you choose.

Consider this scenario. You're at home arguing with your partner. Arguing fiercely, even. The telephone rings. You pick it up, smile sweetly, and politely greet the caller. When you've finished you put down the phone, turn around and off you go again in combat mode. I'm not encouraging or endorsing such behaviour but I use it to demonstrate just how easily you can switch emotional and mental channels. It's no more difficult than pressing a button on the remote control of your television. So, knowing that you have the power to be in basically whatever mood you choose should give you a hint as to how you can control your thoughts and actions. The secret here is always choosing a channel that'll work for you. You can choose the business channel, the caring channel, the aggressive channel, the family channel, or the victim channel. In fact, we are all likely to use multiple channels throughout our life. Just recognise that *you* have the remote control—nobody else.

Tomorrow morning when you get out of bed you now know that you can choose your mood, thoughts and channel. You can choose to be positive or negative. Being positive will very likely make your day interesting, productive, useful and exciting. Or you can choose to be pessimistic—a popular channel—which is likely to bring very little productivity. If you find yourself on the wrong channel, try switching across. Sometimes something puts you on the wrong

YOU DON'T HAVE TO BE BORN BRILLIANT

track, almost without you noticing it happen. Someone cuts you off in the traffic, someone says something hurtful—and you find yourself on the wrong wavelength. Simply switch back. Say to yourself, 'I'm going to switch back to Channel 37, now'.

When I leave for the office in the morning I'm usually fired up from exercising and listening to my favourite music, but occasionally I still have an unproductive thought in my mind. To combat this I've adopted a ritual. As I turn the key to my car ignition on, I mentally switch on Channel 37, the positive channel, and Channel 39, the business channel. I tell my subconscious that now is the time to switch into positive, business mode so I can enjoy the day and be more productive. It might sound like a fantasy, but I can tell you, it works every time. Then I crank up music that gets me excited and I'm off to work.

In essence, we are what we think. This is why it's so important to take control of our thoughts: to trawl through them and eradicate those that are negative and therefore useless; to keep feeding into our minds more and more positive thoughts.

Another way to do this is by affirmations—that

is, by implanting positive thoughts in our minds by repeating them over and over to ourselves. I say to myself every day: 'The world is a great place full of opportunities' and 'Everything that comes my way is a gift'. Even if I don't say them out loud, I still think them.

Our thoughts determine our attitude. And in life, attitude is always at the heart of success.

PERSISTENCE

A positive attitude is like a living organism that needs to be nourished and tended every day. You can't just read an uplifting book or go to a motivational seminar and expect to have a positive attitude for the rest of your life, just as you can't have a shower and expect to remain clean and fresh for the rest of your life! So having a great attitude is not a one-off event it's a process that requires daily attention. You may be on track today, but you can be certain that something will happen next week or next month to knock you off track. And when you do get knocked off track you will need some tools to get yourself back on track. These tools might include reading books, listening to tapes, attending seminars or hanging out with positive people.

I motivate myself every day. There are often mornings when I wake up and don't want to get out of bed. I might have twelve meetings lined up that day, most of them tough; a key member of my team may be about to resign; a big deal could be swaying in the wind—who knows what could go wrong? When I feel like this I find listening to motivational tapes a great help. I live only a few minutes' drive from my work, but every day my habit is to either play inspirational music or push in a motivational tape as soon as I turn on the ignition. This way I get my attitude on the right track.

This morning I listened to Michael Dell from Dell Computers. By the age of thirty Michael had built one of the world's biggest companies. The story of how he did it—how he motivates his managers and staff, his key strategies for sales and marketing—makes fascinating listening. This sort of stuff is priceless, and I'm amazed at how many people seem to struggle but refuse to listen to the tapes that could give them the inspiration or information they need.

I also regularly use what I call 'success journals'. These are two books I have created with thick red cardboard covers. One is an album in which I keep photos, letters or memorabilia that I find uplifting. Some of the photos are of me with someone who motivated me, some are just pleasant memories. In my other book I've pasted newspaper and magazine articles, chapters of a great book or just quotes that I've found inspiring. Often, when I have a spare moment, I'll look into the journal and read something I haven't read for three or four years, and invariably it gives me the same positive boost that it gave me when I first read it. I'll also sometimes open the journal before I have to make a key speech, attend an important meeting or do something else that's particularly challenging. I find that if I get my mind-set right before I take on a major challenge it becomes a lot easier.

A positive attitude is like a habit: the longer you have it, the easier it is to maintain. Or like exercising—the more you do it, the easier it becomes. After a while it develops a momentum of its own, and before long you'll find that it's harder to think negatively than to think positively. Whenever a problem arises, I now automatically look for a solution that can turn the negative into a positive and move on.

FOCUS ON WHAT YOU CAN CONTROL

Rather than try to fix the outside world around you, fix what's inside. You have total control of what's inside, whereas you don't have control of what's outside. If you're having trouble with a relationship, you can't control what your partner does in the relationship, but you can control what you do. And if you change the way that you interact in the relationship, the chances are your relationship will change, too. So instead of pointing the finger at your partner (or boss or parents or whoever), look at yourself and ask what you could do to change the situation.

I remember when I started my business in 1989. The economy was spiralling downward and my friends and family were very concerned for me, starting a brand new business in such a volatile environment. Interest rates on business loans were at 17%, the real estate market was falling and economists were predicting the toughest five years ahead for a long time. I considered their warnings and looked at the environment. They were right. I couldn't control the interest rates, market or confidence. Things in those areas were challenging, and history now tells us that many businesses, both established and new, did fall at that time.

I couldn't control those things but I *could* control a range of other things. I could control the quality of my marketing. I had total control over my attitude, commitment and passion. I could deliver great training to my team and ensure that I only recruited the best people. These things seemed so much more critical to my success path than the external elements. I never allowed a negative or doubtful thought to enter my mind. Admittedly I was probably running on a mixture of naivety and enthusiasm, but it really didn't matter—what mattered was that I believed I could do it and gave myself every possible chance by investing all my energy into things I knew I could control.

I think of my life as divided into two zones, an inner circle surrounded by a broad outer band. The outer band consists of things which may affect me in some way but which are beyond my control—things like interest rates, the seasons, the state of the economy, competition and politics.

The inner circle consists of things over which I have control: my attitude, my goals, the time I wake up, my health, the hours I work each day, the number of books I read. My advice is to focus on the inner circle of influence. Every day act upon what you can control. Don't waste a minute worrying about the rest.

As it happens, the things that you control happen to be the things that really make a difference in life. And the things you can't control happen to be things that don't really affect you in the long run. Whether or not you're passionate, focused and organised will ultimately have a far greater impact on your life than the rise or fall of interest rates!

Learning: The most important factor in enabling you to achieve a magnificent life is a great attitude. If you become a black belt of the mind—if you create beliefs that will empower your results, not limit them—you'll very quickly be able to make your world into whatever you would like it to be.

PART 2

Creating a Life Plan

Sliding doors

Did you ever see the movie *Sliding Doors*? I'm a big fan of the cinema—it's one of my favourite pastimes. I watch movies as a release from my hectic schedule, and I also find they often have great lessons hidden within them. I found this was the case with *Sliding Doors*.

If you haven't seen it I won't ruin it for you, but I'll give you a brief synopsis so you can understand the learning. It's about a young woman who is in a relationship. She is in love with her partner and sees the relationship as long term. One day she heads off to work. At a particular point on her commute she's getting onto her train at the exact moment the door is starting to slide shut. What follows is a fascinating split-story of how different her life and relationship turn out, dependent upon whether she makes the door before it closes or not.

The metaphor is a strong one. Every day that you rise to greet this magnificent world there is an abundance of opportunity surrounding you. Opportunity to be creative, to go the extra mile, to be a giver, to learn, to advance your career and your ability to take advantage of this opportunity depends on whether you 'step through the doors' or miss them altogether. Just think, the next telephone call you take could be someone who could change your life—a new customer, old friend, mentor or even life partner. Yet many people answer the telephone as though it were an annoying distraction. Therefore a life-changing opportunity could come and go without you even noticing it.

So how do you capitalise? You answer every call as though it could change your life—with enthusiasm, excitement and an 'It's my pleasure' attitude. You greet every person you come across as a friend you haven't got to know yet. See every meeting as though it will be a catalyst for something great. You never let yourself be anything other than your best.

By doing these things no matter what opportunities cross your path you'll be in a great position to capitalise on them.

RAISING THE BAR

This really leads us into the question of standards. Whether you realise it or not, you have a set of standards which you maintain in every area of your life: career, health, relationships, customer service. Many of us don't even realise we have these standards, but we do. Take punctuality: you either have a standard of being on time or you keep people waiting. Relationships: you either nurture and support your partner or you don't. Food management: you either eat food that nourishes you or you eat whatever is served to you. They're all standards.

One simple way to enhance the quality of your life instantly is to review these standards and raise them to the roof. I'll give you an example. Remember back to when you had your first date with someone you were very attracted to. It may have been with your current partner, or someone from the past. Think about how well you prepared yourself. My guess is you might have had your hair cut or styled the day before, pressed your favourite outfit, chosen a wonderful restaurant, cleaned your car, been ready an hour early, given your date sincere compliments and so on. Most of us can relate to such an experience. Now, chances are your date was a great success. The reason for this is that you put thought and effort into it—you were excited and did everything possible to deliver a great experience. You set high standards.

For many people, if the relationship developed and indeed matured the standards exhibited on the first date could have dropped. They would not be planning as many exciting adventures after several months. Their punctuality may not be up to scratch. There'd be no more love letters or small spontaneous gifts. Basically, there'd be a general lowering of standards. Not surprisingly, many such relationships fizzle out as they mature. It's not really the time span that causes the magic to fade—it's a change in standards. I'm not saying that every night needs to be like your first date, but if you approach the relationship more along those lines it's bound to reach a much deeper and far more exciting level than if you don't.

Similarly, think about your first day of work at a new job. I bet you were there early, looking your best and ready to impress. There was a certain freshness and excitement about what lay ahead. You would have been looking for opportunities to take on more work and add value to the company that had given you this great opportunity. Some time down the track that enthusiasm might have faded away. Imagine if you arrived at work in this fashion every single day—how much of a difference would that make to your career?

There's an old saying that the one great advantage of being mediocre is that you're always at your best. It's a joke, yet it's true. Many prefer the comfort zone of mediocrity to the excitement zone of aiming high.

Few of us will ever find success in the comfort zone. We'll find it only by constantly stretching ourselves to new limits. When we stretch ourselves, we normally don't then return to where we previously were. Once we manage to perform at this higher level, the chances are we'll continue to perform at that level forever. It's by attaining these higher standards that you raise the level of your performance and quality of your life.

What does this mean in a practical sense? How do you go about raising standards in your everyday life? The answer is to do it systematically and do it now. Break down your life into its main components and see how you can improve on each of them. Your working hours is an obvious example. You could decide that from now you're going to work an extra half an hour every day by getting up an hour earlier each morning. Or if you're a salesperson who's used to making ten calls on an average a day, you could decide that from now on you'll average fifteen. Or if you're a boss who's not been in the habit of giving your staff recognition, you could decide to turn this around. Someone once said that a good boss isn't one who catches people doing things wrong but one who catches people doing things right.

You can raise your standards in your personal life, too. You might decide that every day from now on you'll say something meaningful to your partner that you know will make them feel good. How simple is that—saying one thing a day and it could transform your relationship! Doing small things like this can revolutionise your life, because when you do them often enough they become a habit.

Raising the bar is a good metaphor for improving one's standards, because this is what high jumpers do: they keep raising the bar by continually aiming a bit higher, trying a little harder, jumping a little better. I once read how the Ninja warriors in Japan were trained as children to jump from a standing position. A bamboo shoot was planted for each child, who from that day on had to jump over it each day. At first, when the shoots were only ankle high, there was no difficulty in the task. But as the shoots grew into canes, the children were constantly stretched to new limits but because it was a process of small, daily improvement, it was achievable. Each day, as the cane grew a fraction taller, each child had to jump a little higher to clear it. The constant need to raise their standards meant they ended up jumping over tall canes with surprising ease.

We can apply this metaphor to our own lives. If we can do just a bit extra each day, push a little higher and further, we will end up with a massive improvement.

Learning: One of the fastest ways to change your life is to raise your standards. Live each day as though it was the most exciting opportunity ever provided to anyone on the planet—because it is. Recognise that each and every day there will be numerous events that have the ability to change your life forever. Therefore always be at your best.

MOST PEOPLE AIM AT NOTHING AND HAVE AMAZING ACCURACY AT ACHIEVING IT

Ring up your closest friend. Question a colleague. Ask the next person you meet: 'What do you hope to achieve with your life? What's really important to you?' Or even, 'What are your goals for the next 90 days?'

These are major life questions that you would hope most people could answer with a degree of certainty; yet I guarantee these questions are more likely to draw a blank stare than a clear set of milestones. Here is the beginning of what holds most people back. They just aren't clear enough about what it is that they want to achieve. Today. This week. Or for the rest of their life.

I can relate to the 'no goal-setting' regimen. I did

it myself for a period—superbly! And it worked. No goals, no results! After all, why set goals when they were unlikely to be achieved?

This small poppy philosophy has been drilled into most of us between birth and age 20 in varying degrees. And you can't be blamed for that. But you *can* now draw a line in the sand and realise that you have the opportunity to re-program the most powerful computer in the world—your mind. Forget the past programming that had been encoded by those around you. It's served its purpose; it's got you through those tough early years in one piece. Now decide to replace it with a potent program which will bring you everything you ever dreamed of. Do it right now.

Doesn't it feel good thinking like this? I bet for a moment at least you felt a warmth spread throughout your body as your inner radar got a sense of a new destination—a destination you could reach if you peeled away the subtle layers of negative and conservative thinking that sit atop most of our day-to-day decision-making and thinking.

By the end of this section I expect that you will have completed the most important exercise you can *where to live – Remember! what job to do – Remember!*

ever undertake: the creation of your Life Blueprint. Within a short time from now you will have a simple plan that could amplify the results you have been achieving, tenfold.

But, don't let the simplicity of the task fool you into thinking that the results will be minimal. It is a process that has the capability of jet-propelling your life. <u>If you are crystal clear on where your life's headed it's only a matter of time before you'll arrive.</u> But be careful. Until you have completed your re-programming, what invariably follows such a simple revelation is a barrage of self-doubt creeping back in to your thoughts, your inner voice shouting, 'It can't be that easy—you've had dreams before that you couldn't achieve. Don't bother. Your life is headed for the scrap heap, no matter what!'

I get the same sort of messages that creep into my head every day. It's normal that the part of you that's been set up to protect your feelings (and let's face it, it's been working overtime in most of us) won't disappear instantly—in fact, it may never go away. What you can change, though, is your response. I simply stop, take a breath, know that the negative thoughts are not right and then override them with commitment and intuition. It's a process that can be learnt and perfected instantly. You just need to know that it is not a question of *whether* you can achieve all your goals—it's only a question of *how*. And, depending upon your sense of urgency and ability to implement new strategies, *when*.

So, back to your Life Blueprint. Many of us don't start making a plan because we don't know what should be in it. So let's look at the contents. My Life Blueprint is broken into these two sections:

SHORT-TERM GOALS

Put in this section all the things that you want to achieve in the next 90 days. When I say 'achieve', it may well be referring to starting an activity. For example, if you haven't exercised for ten years it'll be hard to put down 'Get fit', but you may put down 'Find a personal trainer, join a gym and exercise for 30 minutes a day, three days a week'.

It should be like an extended 'To Do' list made up of important tasks that, when completed, will

Contact singing teacher. Start lessons
YOU DON'T HAVE TO BE BORN BRILLIANT
Go Diving regularly — check out Diving club.

enhance the quality of your life. It could include reading a certain book, improving your diet, or calling someone important to you. Anything.

And keep it simple. Each goal need only be a few words. When you see the words written you'll know exactly what's required. Try to put down at least ten things that you are committed to achieving in the next three months. If you hit 75 per cent of them your life will be radically different. Not only will those specific areas have improved dramatically but you'll also find that there's a ripple effect, like dropping a pebble into a pond: the ripple starts at the spot you dropped the pebble but soon extends to the outer sections of the pond. The same works in your life: start to get fit and people notice; they make positive comments and your self-esteem increases. As your confidence increases you make better-quality decisions and act with more certainty. One success leads to another three. So, identify several areas to upgrade. Jot them down and take action immediately. Notice I didn't say soon or next week. It must happen while you're in a state of inspiration. If you're excited about something, start it now. It's the starting that's usually the most difficult part. Once you're

Impress Charles at work
Improve my diet — eat more of things that are good for me & less of

Walk every day on the beach.

on a roll and developing momentum the results tend to increase as the effort decreases.

LONG-TERM GOALS

Here's where you'll put down the larger milestones that are important to you but unlikely to manifest in the next 90 days. One of my major life goals is to be Prime Minister of Australia—which is not going to happen in 90 days, but the mere presence of the goal will set up my internal radar, seeking opportunities to get closer to it. This is actually a biological phenomena as well as a commonsense approach. Within your brain there's a tiny area called the reticular activating system (RAS). This incredibly important tool allows you to subconsciously filter out things that aren't important to you and focus on those that are.

I'll give you an example. A sleeping parent could be subjected to loud outside noises, such as peoples' voices, traffic noise or the television, without it disturbing their sleeping pattern. But the faintest sound of their baby stirring several rooms away will get their immediate attention amidst this sea of noise.

things that aren't

Or if you have no children you might relate to the scenario where you've made your decision to buy something. Let's say a car. And suppose you woke up and decided you were going to buy a white BMW. Guaranteed on your way to work that morning every third car whizzing past you will be a white BMW! Not literally, but it appears that way. Why? Because your RAS now knows what you're looking for and alerts you to anything which may be useful in achieving that goal.

In the same way, writing a list of goals doesn't materially affect the external world the minute your list is complete, but what does happen is you now know what's important and you can easily identify interesting opportunities.

Try this. Think of something you're challenged with. Write it down and concentrate on it. Now list several things that could be of use in achieving the outcome you want.

Say your challenge was that you wanted to lose weight. Write a list of things that could help you undertake the challenge—fit friends, health-food shop, gymnasium, jogging track, dietary information, running shoes. Then see what happens. I guarantee that within 24 hours, some of these things will have come into your life like magic. How? I don't really know—they just do. To this day I have no real understanding of how electricity is made, transported and stored, but I switch on lights all the time. You don't really have to understand how these things work—you simply have to get them working for you.

STEPS TO GOAL SETTING

Okay, so you know what should go into your Life Blueprint, but you're having trouble identifying your goals. Don't worry. If you've never set any goals in your life, in five minutes you will have! Just follow these seven steps.

1. **Identify your goals.** This can be done in a brainstorming session, alone or with your partner. Don't sell yourself short, and don't let anyone else do it for you. We often tend to aim low out of fear of failure.
2. **Write down your goals in order of importance and achievability.** The process of writing your

goals down rather than keeping them in your head makes them real. Prioritising them also programs your mind to seek opportunities relating to your most important goals first.

I start off each morning with a list of maybe ten things to do and spend a few minutes prioritising the list. There's usually something on it which is so important that if I did that and nothing else I could consider my day to have been successful. If so, I do it first. If I don't get to the bottom of the list by the end of the day, I don't worry. What's at the bottom will be less important. The truth is that at least a third of the things we do each day are of such little importance that if we didn't do them at all it would make no difference to our lives. I sometimes turn up to-do lists which I made six months before and which contain items I never crossed off—that is, things I never did. But not doing them made no difference to my life at all.

3. **Put a time stamp on your goals.** Even if you're not sure how long it will take to achieve any one goal, set a sunset clause. This takes a goal from being a concept to a project.

4. **Work out what key actions are needed to achieve each of your goals.** Let's say your ambition is to open a shop. Your actions might then be to 1) research the nature of the business, 2) visit the best operator in the field, 3) work out the finances required, 4) take steps to acquire more experience in the field if this is needed, and so on. Arrange these actions in order of importance.
5. **Review regularly what progress you're making.** As you do, keep this important fact in mind: achieving success isn't a perfect science. I used to think it was. I thought you had to complete step one before step two, and two before three. With experience I've come to realise that the most important thing is just to get started somewhere. It's a bit like having to have a challenging conversation with someone. Many of us do nothing while we agonise over how to broach the subject. Better to just start talking to the other person—'Hey, I'd like to have a chat with you about…'—and allow the conversation to work its own way to the matter at hand.
6. **Regularly review the goals.** This is a longer-term exercise. It's necessary because the goals you set

for yourself today may not be the goals you'll be wanting to strive for twelve months from now.

ACCOUNTABILITY

Another good reason for writing down your goals is so that you can give them to other people. If you write the list and put it in the top drawer, there's every chance you'll forget about it. But if you give a copy to two or three people who are close to you the list will take on a life of its own. Why? Because it's a lot easier to let yourself down than to let others down.

We let ourselves down all the time. We make an appointment to go to the gym at 7 p.m. on Thursday but decide to pull out at the last moment. It's a very easy thing to do. But if we arrange to meet a friend there at 7 p.m., the chances are we'll keep the appointment, because it's easier to go to the gym than to let down the friend.

I have found accountability to be an extremely useful tool in strengthening our new patterns of behaviour generally. Being held accountable not just by yourself but by four others, say, your wife or husband, and your three closest friends can give you the extra impetus you need to attain your goals.

Letting other people know what your goals are is essentially a way of keeping yourself honest. Some people might argue that we ought to be able to pursue our goals on our own. That's true: we *should* be able to do it on our own. But most of us can't. We're all fallible; we all have weaknesses. The more support you can get to keep yourself on track the better, and when you let other people know what your goals are you're giving yourself that extra support.

If you're introverted by nature and the idea of telling other people your goals goes against the grain, you'll probably get more out of the exercise than anyone else. I talk from personal experience because I'm a naturally shy and private person away from the business environment. I don't like going to social functions because I never feel comfortable there. If I arrive at a function and find I don't know anyone, my instinct is to turn around and leave. Socially, I've never felt comfortable meeting people I have not met before. I still don't. Yet I've been able to make a habit of sharing goals and have benefited tremendously from it.

How do you get over the inhibition? The only way to get over it is to do it. You just have to put up with any embarrassment you might feel. In reality there won't be any embarrassment. On the contrary: you'll probably be surprised at how positively people react when you show them the list. They'll think better of you for doing it and offer support.

Learning: **Develop absolute clarity around what you want in life—know your goals and study them daily. The clearer you are about the things you want to create for yourself the greater your likelihood of success. And don't be concerned about getting your goals perfect initially, you'll more than likely change them many times in the near future—the key is getting started today. It's important to have direction and clarity—flexibility is easy once you've gained momentum.**

Look after the big rocks first

A primary school teacher stood at the front of her class about to conduct a new lesson for the children. Most were 5 or 6 years of age. She asked for their attention and suggested that the lesson she was about teach would be an important one for life.

She then pulled out from under the bench a large glass beaker with a wide mouth and placed it on the bench. The beaker stood about 12 inches tall. Alongside it she placed an ice cream bucket full of rocks, each about the size of her fist. She carefully placed the big rocks inside the beaker. After fitting about ten rocks inside the jar, the next one she placed on top rolled off and hit the bench. There appeared no room for any more rocks in the jar. She then looked up at the class, smiled and asked the question, 'Would you say that I have a full jar?' The children, recognising that clearly no more rocks could be fitted in, nodded in agreement.

She then pulled out another ice-cream bucket which contained a large number of smaller pebbles, each about the size of a pea. The teacher then carefully poured the pea gravel into the jar until there were no more spaces left between the rocks. Before long the pea gravel also overflowed. The same question was put to the class and again they nodded that *this* time the jar was clearly full.

At this, a third bucket was produced. It was full of sand. The teacher poured the sand between the big rocks and the pea gravel until the space was saturated for the third time. The children were amazed at the capacity of the beaker but were uncertain how to answer the teacher's subsequent request: was the jar now full? Before they could answer, a bottle full of water was produced from under the bench and the liquid was poured between the rocks, gravel and sand.

At the end of this exercise the teacher smiled at her class and said that the demonstration was over. 'Now tell me, children, what is the lesson in this exercise?' to which there was silence for a moment.

Then one enthusiastic young boy raised his hand in excitement. 'Miss, I learned that you can often fit a lot more in than you had first thought,' he said with pride.

'Good answer, Robert, but there is another lesson I would like you to discover.'

The young children thought hard again. This time a tiny red-headed girl at the back of the room raised her hand. 'Miss, the lesson for me is that if you didn't put the big rocks in first you wouldn't have been able to fit everything else in. So my learning is to first place in the big rocks.'

The teacher smiled with great pride. 'You are a very clever class. That is exactly the lesson I was seeking.'

Think about the profound nature of that simple lesson when applied to your life. What are your big rocks? What are the most important things in your life? In your job, what are the most important roles you perform? If you can identify the key things and make sure they get the attention they deserve, you will be able to do so much more than you expected.

Let me give you an example. Assume you had no appointments or obligations in your diary for the next 30 days. What would be the most important things for you to do in this time to enrich your life? Some things I might suggest would be to spend quality time with your loved ones. Attend your daughter's school concert. Watch your son play football. Take your partner out for a romantic dinner. Call your parents or, better still, visit them if possible. Exercise three times a week for an hour.

These things could fall into the category of *big rocks*. They are important activities for your life and soul, things that should never be compromised or shunted to the side of your schedule for activities which appear more urgent but in fact are far less important. These big rocks should be the first ones entered into your diary. If you have these things covered, the other stuff will sit around them neatly like the gravel and sand.

Next, consider what are the important actions you need to handle for work. I know there are a thousand things you could do, but if you could only accomplish, say, ten key tasks at work, what would they be? Training your team? Preparing for a big presentation? Conducting a performance review? Holding a team meeting to share the company's vision? What would be the ten highest pay-off activities? Once you've decided, enter those ten things into your diary alongside the 'appointments' you've already made. That is, within the spaces around your personal big rocks.

By now your diary should be looking quite full. From here, the other things that invariably come up from one day to the next can be slotted in between the appointments in your diary. You see that unless you prioritised the big rocks at work and home you would have been struggling to allocate them the time they require—a bit like putting the sand or water in the beaker before the rest.

Learning: There are certain key elements of your life that should be given priority over all other activities—these are your Big Rocks. Decide what these Big Rocks are and ensure that they receive focus and attention. When you plan your time and decide on your key activities for the upcoming week, place these things in your schedule first—whatever else you fit into your life thereafter is a bonus.

GET ORGANISED, NOW!

I believe that much of your success in life won't come out of being brilliant or incredibly innovative—it'll come from just being plain organised. And to achieve this I suggest you develop several very simple systems as outlined in this chapter. When's a good time to implement them? Today! So let's get started.

ADOPTING A SYSTEM

The McDonald's hamburger chain is a good example of how well a system can work. McDonald's may not make the best burgers in the world, but they are certainly the world's most successful burger company. The reason for this is that they've created a brilliant system for making their burgers, one which ensures consistency of product. The burgers are produced rapidly in large quantities, and each is the same in quality as all the others, almost without fail. By ensuring this, McDonald's hit upon one of the keys to success in business: maintaining consistency of product or service at a high level through systems.

We can transfer the McDonald's experience to our own lives. This simply means creating systems or routines that we can follow instead of reinventing the process every time. Systems and routines are the grease that allows the wheels of our daily lives to keep turning efficiently.

When I go to a routine sales presentation, there are certain things which I need to research beforehand and certain things which I need to take with me. Therefore I have a checklist for sales presentations to make sure everything is covered. It's the same when I go travelling. I nearly always need to take the same things on the same type of trip, so I have a simple checklist for each type of trip to ensure I don't forget anything. That way I also don't have to reinvent the list—cord to the computer battery, business cards, diary, mobile phone—every time I go travelling. Some people might think this is a regimented, un-spontaneous way to live your life. It's not: it's just organised.

And because checklists spare you the worry of remembering everything that needs to be done, they actually free up your mind and make it possible for you to think and act far more spontaneously. When you arrive at the sales presentation, you have nothing else on your mind except making a brilliant presentation. You know you've done the research, you know you've brought everything along. Without a checklist, the chances are that when you start to speak you'll find yourself thinking, 'Gee, did I forget my order form?' If you're thinking like this, you can't possibly be as comfortable making the presentation and therefore you won't be totally focused.

We can introduce system into our lives in all kinds of ways. Take something as simple as locating your car keys. How many of us keep misplacing our keys? I certainly used to. I'd come home and toss them onto a couch or leave them in the kitchen and then waste time wandering about the place trying to find them. Now I put them in the same corner of the same drawer in the same wardrobe every time. They're never lost. How simple! Yet it took me years to adopt it.

Shopping at the greengrocer's is another example most of us are familiar with. It's a time-consuming exercise. You have to drive to the greengrocer, wander about deciding what to buy, then queue to be served. This seemed to me a needless waste of time. So I worked out what fruit and vegetables I went through a week and placed a standing weekly home-delivery order with an Internet site called greengrocer.com.au. This system probably saves me an hour a week. If I ever need to vary the order, I simply do it on the Internet.

I have since introduced systems into my life in other, less conventional ways. I know nothing about fashion. I can never tell which shirt goes with which suit and which tie with which shirt. At the same time, I know that if you're dealing with customers, appearance is important. This is how I got over the problem: I laid out all my clothes, brought in a fashion consultant and got her to decide what went with what. Then I had a photographer come in and take pictures of all the possible combinations, which I now have pinned beside my wardrobe. I wanted to avoid wasting five minutes every morning agonising over what to wear and then inevitably making a mistake. Now I refer to the pictures and immediately the problem is solved. Some people might think this is taking system too far. What I know is that it works and saves time.

Personally, I place a lot of emphasis on preparing myself each night for the next day. My clothes are set out, ready to be worn, and I have a 'to do' list prepared for the next morning, so when I walk into the office I can start work without a moment's delay. I even make a point each night of parking my car rear-first into the garage. Next morning I don't want to be bothered with three-point turns: I want to be able to make a flying start. It's a small thing, maybe, but it helps to create the right mental attitude.

Who wants to spend two minutes a day looking for car keys? Who wants to spend five minutes each morning deciding what to wear and then getting it wrong? Who wants to needlessly spend time shopping for fruit and vegetables? Time-wasting activities can be avoided by systemising your life. The time saved is better invested elsewhere.

KEEPING TABS ON TIME

Some people work for fifteen hours a week and hang out at the office for another forty-five. Usually, these people have no idea they're wasting so much time. On the contrary, the fact they're spending sixty hours a week in the office gives them a feeling of righteousness. They like to think of themselves as world champion of long hours. What they ought to be is world champion of productivity.

It follows then, that awareness of how you're spending your time is a high priority. Awareness requires self-examination. If you're reading this and haven't ever considered the matter, stop now and quiz yourself about it. Am I really productive? Or am I merely in the office all those hours? Other people, by contrast, are aware that their many hours in the office are largely unproductive, yet don't know what to do about it. These people go to work each day, spend eight, ten or more hours at the office, then go home feeling they haven't really achieved anything. If you feel like this, maybe you should have a closer look at how you occupy those hours. The best way to start is to keep a 15-minute log of what you do during the day: that is, make a brief note every 15 minutes of how you've spent the previous 15 minutes.

When you've logged yourself for a few days, analyse your notes to see if you've been doing things which aren't necessary or produce little value—things you'd be better off not doing. If you've been feeling unfulfilled at work, there's every chance you'll find that many of the things you do each day fall into this category. Once you've identified these, try to work out how you can avoid doing them in future. You may find you can eliminate many of them by simply learning to say no, whether to the colleague who wants to waste your time chatting, or a friend who wants to call you five times a day.

An inability to say no is a key reason why many people waste so much time. Another example of this behaviour is not being able to refuse to take a call that they know will interrupt what they're doing. This is why I never take calls as they come in. I batch them up and return them all at once. That way, I can work for three hours uninterrupted and then allocate an hour to returning calls. The alternative is to be taking calls every five minutes, which must reduce your working output to a fraction of what it could be.

The ability to say no is actually an empowering one. By being able to say no you're taking control. You're also freeing up your time to do the things which are necessary and which produce value.

When I recommended this type of time management to someone recently he said, 'I couldn't do that—I've got too many appointments.' I replied, 'Pretend for a minute that you don't have any appointments. Mentally wipe your slate clean. Now, starting with an imaginary blank diary in front of you, what are the six most important things in your business life next week?' He rattled off half a dozen things, and I got him to write them down on a piece of paper divided into five columns, one for each day. I then invited him to check this against his real diary. I suggested he would find that he would have to make room in the diary for the six important things by getting rid of some of the less important appointments. A few he could simply cancel. Others he could delegate to someone else.

LEARNING TO DELEGATE

Another way to free up your time is to delegate. Very often you think you can do a job better than another person, so you do it yourself. Perhaps you *can* do it better than the other person, but often that doesn't matter. If the person you delegate a task to does the job with an 80 per cent satisfactory outcome instead of the 95 per cent outcome you might have achieved yourself, that will probably be good enough. And the reality is that unless you do delegate you'll never grow your business or have time for the important parts of your personal life.

Delegation is an art in itself. It isn't just a case of asking someone to do something you don't have time to do. It's a skill that involves explaining or showing someone exactly what you would like done. If you're moving into a position where you need to delegate, you should first find out the basics by speaking to people with experience at delegating. I still haven't mastered the skill 100 per cent, although I'm a lot better at it than I used to be. At first I was terrible. My main mistake was not spending the time to communicate clearly what I wanted done. I'd simply say, 'Can you go and do that,' without detailing what was required. The usual result was that the person would go away and do a variation of what I wanted done, which invariably led to frustration and tension. Now I take the time to communicate things in more detail.

The other big mistake people make in delegating is that they fail to delegate enough. The downside of this is that you miss out on the time you need to do the really important things that only you can do.

In other words, you end up doing the things you can delegate and failing to do the things you can't.

THE IMPORTANCE OF ROUTINE

A regular routine is an extremely valuable aid in time management. It allows you to maximise your output in the time available. I try to follow a regular routine. I get up at the same time, exercise at the same time, arrive at the office at the same time, typically have my meetings at the same times and even send my e-mails at the same time. Some people might regard a regular routine as restrictive and confining. In fact, it's the reverse: it gives you tremendous freedom. By noon each day I can usually do whatever I want because everything important that I had to do has already been done. So if I wanted to go to the beach or spend the afternoon reading a book, I could do it. My regular routine has enabled me to get through all the essentials in a disciplined fashion by lunchtime, and if some crisis suddenly arose, none of these would be left undone.

EMBRACING TECHNOLOGY

The changes which technology has produced in the last few years is incredible. In the early 1970s, when I was in primary school, the only way you could communicate in writing was by typing a letter on a typewriter, folding it, putting it in an envelope, sending it through the mail and hoping for a response within a week.

By the time I started work in the early 1980s, word processors had come in, so at least it was possible to get the letter out faster. But faxes were still largely unknown. Our real estate office didn't have one; few offices did. When the fax did become popular shortly after this, it allowed us to get a fast letter sent faster. Then came email, which allowed us to deliver the letter faster than by fax. In the space of about 20 years, technology had condensed the time it took to write to a customer and get a written reply from one week or more to a matter of minutes.

There are countless examples of how rapidly the world has been changing. In terms of time management, what does all this mean? It means we should be able to perform at much higher levels than we used to which is exciting. We can all benefit enormously from leading-edge technology, so we should welcome it and embrace it as a friend. There is nothing about technology that we need fear.

Some people fear they'll be unable to cope with new technology. The very mention of words such as Internet, email and databases scares them. Instead of backing off, however, they should be surging forward. They should see the new technology as an exciting opportunity. Socially, intellectually and financially, the new technology has opened fantastic new worlds for all of us.

GETTING THE MOST OUT OF YOUR WORKING DAY

People are at their best at different times of day. Some peak in the afternoon or evening. My guess is, though, that most of us are at our best in the morning. I'm one of these. In the morning I have more energy and I'm able to keep a sharper focus. It's also a fact that once an office gets into full swing, usually around 9 a.m., there are a lot more distractions for everyone.

This is why I find my most productive time of day is from 7 a.m. to 9 a.m. It's a time for me to get things done, and by the end of it I've usually managed to do four hours' work in two.

Most of us can all tell which time of day is best for us personally, and we should try to allocate the day's most important tasks during that time. If morning is your best time, you may choose to leave all your calls to the afternoon. Returning calls doesn't usually require as sharp a focus as preparing business strategies or meeting customers.

For many people, starting work early just isn't an option, perhaps they have family commitments. Some people also say they perform better later in the day and in the evening. If this is true for you, that will be the time when you get most done. But if you're one of those people who say, 'I'm no good in the morning,' make sure you're being honest with yourself: maybe you just don't like getting out of bed!

Whatever time you start, how many hours a day should you work? It's a contentious question. My view is that in the modern competitive business environment it's hard to get ahead working nine to five. Working nine to five earns you a wage. Working slightly longer opens up the possibility of greater success.

I work twelve hours a day—from 7 a.m. to 7 p.m.—six days a week. I don't suggest everyone should do the same. It's a matter of personal choice. I do suggest, though, that you consider 'going the extra mile'—that is, working a little harder than you previously have.

It comes back to feeling enthusiastic and passionate about what you do. This is how I feel about my work: each morning I can't wait to get into the office. For me, work is fun. Someone I know once said to me I was crazy working over 60 hours a week. I asked him what his own working hours were. 'Nine to five,' he said. I asked if he liked his job. He said no, he hated it. I said to him, 'You're the crazy one. You work eight hours a day and hate it. I work twelve hours a day and love it. That's not crazy.'

Some people take the view that it's one thing to turn up for work early if you're a manager, but it's another entirely if you're an ordinary wage-earner. You hear people say: 'Once I get promoted to a managerial position, *then* I'll start getting to work early. Until then, I'll work nine to five.' They fail to see that if they put in the extra effort now they'll probably be promoted more rapidly.

In my company, most of the team work the same hours as me. This includes not only the commission-earning salespeople, whom you might expect to put in longer hours since potentially it means they earn more money. It also includes people on fixed salaries who are paid to work from nine to five. They're there because they enjoy what they do. They want to get ahead; they understand the concept of going the extra mile.

When you enjoy what you do, you don't need to be pushed or reminded to do it. Conversely, if you find it hard to get to work early, or even on time, it's usually because there's no enthusiasm for your job.

So, how do you fix the problem? One way is to switch to a job that you enjoy. For most of us, this is easier said than done. The alternative is to learn to love the job that you have. And how do you do that? Easy. By changing your attitude to it. By finding a way to make it challenging and stimulating.

After leaving school I took a job letterbox dropping to earn extra money. Most people who drop pamphlets hate doing it. They drag themselves around the streets in the heat of the day feeling bored. I found a way of loving it: I wore earphones and listened to music and carrying a backpack with all my pamphlets, I did the rounds early in the morning when the air was crisp and the sun still low. I talked to people along the way. I made it fun. It's easy to be successful at something you enjoy. It's extremely difficult to be successful at something for which you feel no passion at all.

MAKING RULES FOR YOUR IDEAL WEEK

If you don't schedule the important things in your weekly diary rest assured a myriad of insignificant requests, actions, distractions and routine activities will quickly fill up your time.

So I suggest you write out a list of the most important activities for your week—the things that, if completed successfully, will have the greatest impact on your life. The list could include exercise, time with your kids, preparing for an important meeting, reading a life-changing book, writing a business plan. Or it could include having a meeting with your boss to discuss a great new idea you've thought of, or calling up someone for a potential new business relationship. Whatever activities are important for you, list them down.

Then select the day and time within your week when these things would best be handled. And simply make an appointment with the activities (or people). It may sound funny to make an appointment with a task, but it's critical that you do. Many people in the work environment make appointments all day every day with people and find at the end of the day or week their important tasks are left undone.

Once you've got a sense of the regular key activities you have to handle, start developing a regular routine with some key disciplines within it. For example, these are some of the rules I have for my work diary:

- I don't make appointments before midday—that way I know that I have five hours in the morning to handle important tasks without distraction.
- I batch all my appointments together so I can move quickly from one to another without having

to travel back to the office. I may line up four or five appointments in one area at short intervals.
- I also group my key regular activities, such as returning telephone calls and emails. I usually do these at the beginning of each day, after lunch and before I go home. I also only look at my incoming mail once a week: that way it doesn't distract me on a daily basis. Having said that, I do have someone who checks it for me to make sure there's nothing in it that must be attended to more quickly.
- I have appointment-free days each Wednesday and Friday. That allows me to do two things. Firstly, I give myself time to follow up important outcomes from my appointment days (Monday, Tuesday and Thursday). And secondly, I get time to work *on* my business, rather than always working *in* it. I also have a folder on my desk for work that I intend to do on my two days out of the office. So if something comes in which I plan to handle on those days, it goes straight into the folder and I forget it until then.
- I basically have an open-door policy at work for my team. But I have trained my team to come

to me only if they need me, to ask me direct questions that usually only require extensive feedback or direction rather than me doing the thinking for them. I would probably get over 50 questions or requests from my team each day but each one is usually dealt with in under a minute.

SIMPLIFY YOUR LIFE

I'm speaking literally here, not metaphorically. Life is complex enough without hoarding lots of unnecessary baggage. I suggest you take a careful look at what's important to you right now—who's important to you and what you love doing. Once this is done you may want to consider scrutinising the rest and filtering out or reducing what's not important.

Because there appears to be endless choice in virtually any area you look at, people often try to have everything—and in the process become confused, overwhelmed and fearful of making the wrong choice. Let me give you some examples. How many investment opportunities are there in existence? Thousands, if not millions. You have any number of shares, different types of property, funds, ostrich farms—the list goes on. And there are plenty of people hawking around any number of 'get rich' schemes. It's really quite a minefield. If you let it be.

I have a very simple investment philosophy. First, I don't co-invest with other people—that is, I don't joint invest. That way I'm never in conflict with a friend or colleague as to what to do with an investment. If I like it I keep it; if I don't, I liquidate it…in *my* time. Next, I only invest in three things—property, shares and my business. So when someone comes along with a 'fantastic opportunity for me to make quick money', I don't give it any headspace or time. Have I ever missed a good opportunity through having such a focused investment strategy? Of course I have. But the time I would have wasted looking at all these opportunities would have distracted me from my main business interests.

Let's look at something more personal. Friends, and social life. I have a small number of close friends. About 12, to be exact. I love seeing them and care for them dearly—they make my life so much richer. But I also run a growing business six days a week, invest time each day in my health and fitness, like to catch up with my family when I can, and enjoy time by myself. And when I fit all those things into my life and allow 7 to 8 hours for sleep, I can tell you I can't find sufficient quality time to spend with more than a dozen friends.

By contrast I have a close friend who is very social. She seems to have an endless list of friends and acquaintances (I swear she must have had to purchase more memory for her computer to store their names). And she's forever struggling to keep in contact with all of them to the point that I see her worn out by the end of the week in the process. She has a totally admirable and wonderful intention, but I wonder about the quality of the time she spends with each person. In addition, her time for herself is invariably compromised in pursuit of pleasing others.

I guess the moral of the story is, consider realistically how much time you have available for social pursuits, taking into consideration other things you do. Consider the possibility of spending quality time with your closest and dearest friends rather than chasing the largest Rolodex of friends on your block.

30 DAYS CAN MAKE A DIFFERENCE

I organise my life with a 30-day planner. It's basically a list of all the things that I need to do, that I need to do better or that I need to keep doing over the next 30 days. Why 30 days? It's a sizeable segment of your year, but it isn't so long that you can't see through to the end of it. It's a manageable period.

As we've seen before, many people have the notion that if they wait long enough their fortune will change and that something great will happen to them. Except for a minority of people, great things rarely happen to us unless we make them happen. Using a planner is a simple mechanism for doing this. It serves as an instruction manual for the next 30 days of your life. It gives you a daily focus. It makes you accountable. It enables you to measure what success you're achieving. It lets you identify those areas in which you're letting yourself down.

Without a planner, you're likely to meander and underachieve. With a planner, it's all but impossible *not* to achieve.

The planner can also be used to shape your personal behaviour. Let's say you feel you're overly critical by nature. Make it an item in your planner that you refrain from speaking badly about anyone. You'll have a much better chance of doing this if it's there, written on the page.

My planner consists of a spreadsheet divided into the 30 days, in which I list the objectives I've set myself. (If you don't have a spreadsheet, an A4 sheet of paper will do.) I list the things in my life that I need to do or do better to achieve my goals and tick them off one day at a time. Let's imagine that on day one I've written 'Exercise for 30 minutes.' If I do the exercise, I tick the item on the list. If I don't, I leave it unmarked. And so on. After seven days or so, it's obvious from the spreadsheet that I've done only two of the five exercise sessions I planned for myself. At a glance I can tell how I'm faring.

Note that it isn't your goals you list in the planner but, rather, the actions you need to take to achieve those goals. Your goal may be to shed 5 kilograms, but what you list in your planner may be: 'Walk for twenty minutes' or 'Eat fruit for breakfast'. Your goals are the big landmarks that you're heading towards. What goes into the planner are the day-to-day things you have to do to get there.

What's the purpose of all this? It's breaking your life into bite-sized segments that you can monitor and control. It's a simple strategy, but it works. There are probably four or five areas in your daily routine that, if you changed them, would massively upgrade your life, so concentrate on these. One might be to improve your fitness. So let's start with 20 minutes' exercise a day, and let's do it three days a week. That's the action—write it down. Another might be to cut back on alcohol. Let's resolve to have five alcohol-free days a week and to have no more than two drinks on the other days. That's another action—write it down.

Before leaving this chapter, let me reiterate that having things on paper is a big plus. Once you write something down, it's always there to be referred to. If you don't put it on paper, the chances are you're going to be swamped by the multitude of ordinary events that fill your day and you won't remember what you resolved to do to improve your life. If you do have your list of actions on paper, they're there to be reviewed at the end of the day and, even if it's been a bad day and you've failed to do most of what you set yourself, you can get yourself back on track merely by reviewing them.

Learning: **Being organised—creating scaffolding to support the key activities of your life—is crucial to your success. Everyone in the world has 24 hours at their disposal each day. What sets apart the highest achievers is what they do with that time.**

First we make our habits then our habits make us

Do you realise that about 75% of the actions you take and the thoughts you have are actually habitual. Think about it. You get up at about the same time every day. You take a shower and do the same routine every day. You eat the same food, drive the same way to work, listen to the same radio station, arrive at work at the same time, say the same thing when you arrive, eat the same lunch etc etc. Marvellous actually that your body and mind have developed the ability to do so much on auto-pilot.

Take driving for a moment. When you first learned it was probably quite challenging. You had to think about everything you were doing with incredible intensity and even then you were likely to screw up much of what you were doing. You had to think about the traffic signals, when to indicate, how to bring the car to a smooth stop. Each was a conscious action. But if you've been driving for a while it's probably second nature today. In fact you probably never have to think how to get where you're going, when to indicate or any of those things any longer. You just do it. And at the same time most people are either on a mobile phone call, listening to a talk back radio station or mentally preparing for their next meeting. The fact is we've become so used to it we don't even think about the process.

And this can be great. It certainly saves lots of brainpower if you don't have to think too hard about the process of brushing your teeth or tying your shoelace. But the reverse is also true. If the habits that you've developed over the years aren't world-class (and let's face it, there are some pretty mediocre and unusual habits floating around out there) they'll also be holding you back without you noticing it.

Blockages in the arteries of success

Whilst the majority of this book has so far dealt with the concepts that are going to propel you towards more success, I now want to deal with three elements in your life that are most likely to hold you back from it.

If you can eradicate these diseases and develop the skills required, you can literally have whatever you want out of life.

EXCUSES

What are excuses? In their simplest form they're a justification for not achieving a desired outcome, an opportunity to lay blame elsewhere, away from yourself.

I think that you either achieve results or you make excuses; the two rarely exist in the same environment. I know a guy who I think has lots of talent. He's smart and witty and capable of almost anything. Yet for over ten years he's been making excuses for not doing what he could be. I'm not saying he should be aiming for anything in particular, but he consistently declares that he wants to achieve certain outcomes for himself and just as consistently finds multiple excuses for missing the target.

He has caught the disease of excuses. It's become so habitual that you can see the excuse coming a mile off. Whether he's starting a new routine, going for a job or even performing a simple errand, he invariably starts the project and gets to a certain point before finding the nearest excuse to opt out. And the scary thing is that it happens almost effortlessly because he's become so good at it. So all of his talent and skill is going to waste because he fails to see the danger of his excuses.

I teach our team at work that excuses don't serve any purpose whatsoever. You have a goal, create a plan, take action and either hit the mark or don't. If you don't you can either start again in another fashion or make the decision that you're no longer prepared to do whatever it takes to get the result. But don't make excuses. Accept responsibility for the outcome. Own it. Then move ahead.

DISTRACTIONS

I've spoken quite a bit about the simplicity of achievement: the need for clarity, the purpose of a plan, getting started and persisting until you achieve your goal. The formula is not complicated. But we need to be realistic about distractions because we don't live in a vacuum—we live in a real world where we get sick, have relationship challenges, receive thousands of external messages daily, and experience many other things that could be potential distractions.

So we need to consider for a moment how we can contain some of the more common forms of distractions in order to support our progress. And just like excuses, you'll be amazed at just how many of these distractions are controllable. Things you might have always thought lay outside your jurisdiction can be handled if you make the decision to control them.

Let's take a common example: an incoming telephone call. Most people would be distracted many times a day by the telephone. Many of the distractions are admittedly quite pleasant, but if you're focused on a plan and need uninterrupted time to develop it, such calls can be untimely. And in the work environment the number of incoming calls daily can be dozens or more.

I have a couple of simple ways of dealing with such distractions. I share them with you not necessarily to be copied but more to demonstrate that there are ways of taking control. Firstly, I have no home telephone. If I need to make an outgoing call or am expecting an important call in, I switch on my mobile phone (which I rarely have to). The way I look at it, I'm at work between 7.00 a.m. and 7.00 p.m. most days, so there's plenty of time for people to get a message through during those times. When I get home the last thing I feel like doing is fielding calls from whoever feels like calling. I also check my voicemail usually once an evening, so if there is anything urgent I can respond to it, but there's never been anything so far that couldn't wait until the morning. The result for me is that I get the opportunity to spend a few uninterrupted hours at home in the evening relaxing, reading a book, watching a favourite television program or enjoying the company of a friend. It's time I give myself to recharge, think about the day or just lie in a bath.

A second method I have for dealing with the distraction of telephone calls is to batch my calls during the day and return the majority of them at set times or whilst in the car travelling to appointments. In essence, I rarely take incoming calls at work because I usually have multiple projects occurring which need my attention. Think about what other distractions you might have come to accept as part of everyday life, and see what you can do to reduce or even eliminate them.

FEAR

Fear is undoubtedly the major blockage in the arteries of success. Fear of rejection and fear of failure (which could lead to rejection) are major challenges for most people. 'If I try to do that and fail I'll look stupid' is what most people think. The result? They either don't start or don't push themselves to their limit.

I can totally relate to the emotion of fear. As a teenager I had a PhD in it. I was reclusive—afraid to go out and extremely uncomfortable in social situations. I was awkward and lacking in confidence. It was at the age of 20, when I got my first job selling real estate, I realised that if I wanted to be successful at selling I would need to communicate more effectively and confidently with people. I figured that awkward, introverted salespeople would find it tough to get ahead. So I enrolled in a two-month Toastmasters course.

On the first night they gave each of the attendees a big white folder. As I didn't want to meet anyone, I sat in a corner before the class started and pretended to read the folder from cover to cover, hoping all the while that nobody would come up and talk to me. Nobody did, but eventually the teacher came in and said, 'We've got eight weeks together. Sixteen nights, to be precise. The purpose of the course is to make sure that by the end of the course you're comfortable either communicating one to one or speaking to a group. To start with, right now, I'm going to ask you all to stand up and tell us in 60 seconds why you're here.'

It was my worst fear come true. I was sick in the stomach. They hadn't told us that we'd be speaking in front of a group this early! I started to perspire and thought about sneaking out of the room, never to return. But something kept me there despite my pain.

At last my turn came. I stood up, my stomach in knots, and spluttered something about starting a career in real estate. I was still in a daze when I sat down; I was certain I'd made a fool of myself. I went home that night and began to think seriously of not going back the following week. Nobody there knew me, and nobody would have cared less if I didn't show up again. It would have been so easy to go to the movies that night instead... But somehow I got myself back there a week later. Thank God I did.

At the end of the eight weeks I was able to stand up for five minutes and say something to a group of people. Today, I can speak for three or fours hours on stage to thousands of people at a time and love every minute of it. I enjoy the surge of adrenalin it gives me.

That's not to say I don't feel nervous before each speech. Now, though, it's a pleasant nervousness. It's not about whether or not I'm capable of making the speech but whether or not it will be the best speech I've ever delivered. I'm still subject to irrational fears. Sometimes, before going on stage, the thought will come over me that when I get to the microphone my mind may go a complete blank. I'm sure it won't ever happen, but I may never rid myself of this fear.

What's true of making speeches is also true of life in general. You don't have eliminate the fear; you just have to make sure it doesn't stop you from moving forward.

In life, just about every kind of participation exposes you to the risk of embarrassment, ridicule or rejection. Whether you're a concerned citizen wanting to stand for the local council, a migrant wanting to go to English language classes, or an amateur singer wanting to enter a competition, getting involved carries with it a risk of rejection.

In some cases the risk is real. Another recent example of this was when I went to Melbourne in

BLOCKAGES IN THE ARTERIES OF SUCCESS

1999 to compete in the Australasian Auctioneering contest. To win I had to beat 50 of the best auctioneers in Australia and New Zealand.

Now, contrary to what some people think, being a successful auctioneer doesn't require natural talent. I've proven that; I had to *make* myself an auctioneer. I used to attend auctions around Sydney at night after my working day was finished. I'd sit as close as I could to the auctioneer and tape whatever he said on a mini recorder. Then I'd go back to my flat, replay the tapes and make notes on what the auctioneer had said, their words, tone and pace.

After a while I built up a couple of files on auctioneering patter. I had one file containing descriptions of properties that had appealed to me and another file with humorous one-liners that had relaxed the crowd. I learned them all by heart and practised them at home. Every morning I'd practice an auction while I was in the shower. Nobody else could hear me, so it didn't matter that I was hopeless to begin with. Gradually I got better and better at it, and one day I asked my boss if I could do an auction. He agreed.

The auction day came and I was terrible. Not

long after that I did another auction and I wasn't so bad. I did another and I was better again. Before long I was okay at it, and soon after I was quite good. That was 15 years ago. I later discovered that the best auctioneers in the world were in Melbourne. So off I went to Melbourne with my mini recorder and taped the three best auctioneers I could find. I brought the tapes back, wrote down what the auctioneers had said and practised and practised it. By now I was well on the way to mastering the art.

Yet when I went to Melbourne to compete in the Australasian contest I felt as I did on that first Toastmasters night. I had developed a high profile in the real estate industry, so I had a lot to lose. If I didn't make the final it would be embarrassing. On the morning of the competition I sat in my hotel room thinking about it all. I felt so nervous, I thought seriously of pulling out. It would be easy for me to invent some story to explain my late withdrawal: I had to fly back to Sydney to deal with some business crisis or similar. I went down in the lift to the hotel foyer.

The moment that I stepped out of the lift was my moment of decision: would I fly back to Sydney or go to the competition? I decided in that split second to go to the competition. It's in these defining moments in your life—when you have the option to take the easy way out or stay and fight the fear—that you design your future. Recognise these moments and use them to your advantage.

I won my heat that morning and then went on to win the final the following day. And to think I was seconds away from taking the easy way out!

The point of this story is that stress, fear, pain, embarrassment and apprehension are part of life, no matter how old you are or how much success you have achieved. In fact, the more successful you are, the higher the stakes become for you, because people then have a higher expectation of you. They expect you to turn in a top performance every time.

I said earlier that failure is almost always the precursor of major success. There is a reason for that. Nearly every major success requires you at some point to make a leap of faith. To achieve major success you have to take your business or your personal life to a whole new level, and this always involves the risk of failure. If instead you're content to move ahead incrementally with small improvements, you won't run the same risk of failure. But you won't be as likely to achieve major success, either.

It's not just a matter of perceptions. Looking back on my own life, I can say with certainty that I learned much more from the things that went badly for me than from the things that went right. The more problems you have in life, the more experience you gain, the more you grow as a person, the more challenges you learn to overcome, the more you are stretched to higher levels. So don't wish to be spared problems. Wish to be able to turn problems to your advantage, because that's how success is achieved.

All it requires is a mental commitment. Before you turn this page, commit yourself to a new kind of mind-set. From now on, no matter what setbacks you encounter, move to a state of mind which does not dwell on the disappointment but, rather, looks for the gift wrapped within.

PROBLEMS: THEY'RE THERE TO BE SOLVED

We can all learn from successful people.

The other evening I had dinner with an associate of Harry Triguboff, the man who owns Meriton

Apartments. Whether or not you like the design of Meriton buildings, you have to agree that Harry is an extremely successful businessman. He came to Australia with nothing and has made himself a billionaire. As always, I was keen to find out what there was about Harry that made him such a high achiever. As soon as we sat down at the table I said to his associate, 'Tell me about Harry. How come he's been so successful?' He replied that in his view Harry's most important quality was his single-mindedness. 'Harry has a goal and a vision,' he said. 'He walks into a meeting and he doesn't want to hear why we can't do it. He wants to hear how we can do it.'

What is your own default mechanism in this situation? If you find the road blocked by a river, do you automatically think to yourself that there's no way you can possibly go any further? Or do you start working out ways that you can get across the river—maybe by using a raft, or a rope, or a flying fox—assessing each to decide which is the most suitable? Your success in life may well be determined by which way you react to problems.

Here is an essential fact about problems and how they can be solved: *for every one problem there are multiple solutions*. I don't believe there has ever been a problem, anywhere, which couldn't be solved in multiple ways. So the question to be asked when a problem arises is not, 'Can it be solved?' but, rather, 'Which solution do we go with?' This was the point of the story about Harry Triguboff. The idea that a problem might not have a solution obviously does not enter his head. For him, the only question is which solution.

RESILIANCE: RISING ABOVE FAILURE

Another thing we can learn from successful people is resilience. It's one of the outstanding characteristics of such people. Successful people are successful because they realise, either intuitively or through experience, that in life we rarely achieve our goals at the first, second, third or even fifteenth attempt. Typically, the person who is ultimately successful heads down one path but finds it blocked, heads down another which also turns out to be blocked, steps back to reconsider the approach taken, tries a third path which is blocked, and so on until at last they find a way through.

BLOCKAGES IN THE ARTERIES OF SUCCESS

So many times, in so many lives, the wind can suddenly shift. You think you're heading for starboard, then all of a sudden you have to tack to port. Usually, you can't anticipate or avoid events of this kind: you just have to go along with the new direction and make the most of it. If you work for a bank that's decided to lay off 3000 people and you're one of them, there's probably nothing you can do to change that decision. But you can change the way you respond to it. You can see it as a great opportunity and decide to go out and learn a new skill, starting a new career that's better than the former one.

Most people can usually think of any number of reasons why something can't be done. I impress this upon my own team. If one of my managers wants to give me five reasons why we can't do something, I will say, 'I really appreciate that. So I assume that once we find solutions to those five problems we can go ahead and do it.' This is recognising the reality of problem-solving: that for each problem that blocks our way there are a number of solutions, and we only need to come up with one of them to get around it.

My attitude is I never ask my team to do the impossible. I make this clear whenever I recruit someone as a manager. I say, 'You should know I will never ask you to do anything that's impossible. Everything I ask of you will be possible, so I expect it to be done. Not everything will be easy. Not everything will be simple. But everything will be possible.' They come to work every morning knowing that they won't be asked to do anything that day that is beyond them, that there will be a way to get around any problem that arises.

You will never achieve anything worthwhile without paying some price. And most times the price you'll pay comes in the form of failure or pain before success. In fact I don't think I have ever achieved anything in my life that was worthwhile without falling on my face multiple times before reaching the goal line. It's part of the process and part of the learning experience we invariably go through to sure up future success.

I say this because I watch so many people embark upon an important goal or project and often stop short of their desired outcome due to what I would see as temporary setbacks. These are often in the form of rejection or occasionally ridicule, when someone else doesn't buy into their dream or has a different point of view. And they let them steal away their dream by sowing the seed of self-doubt.

It reminds me of a story I heard when I was younger of the man who owned a great piece of land that he heard may have diamonds laying beneath it so he set out to discover his potential fortune. He started digging with great enthusiasm, spurred on by the promise of great riches that would change his life. After each spade full of dirt was raised from the ground he'd look for the precious diamonds. After a full day of digging, with an aching back and feeling fatigued he abandoned his dream and sold the land to his neighbour, thinking it had little value other than for grazing cattle. The neighbour spotted the section of land that had been upturned and wandered down, wondering why the man had left it in such a mess. He saw the shovel that had been thrown down by the side of the digging and decided to upturn some of the soil in an attempt to understand what he had been digging for.

To his amazement the third spade full of earth possessed two glorious rough diamonds staring up at him. You see the previous owner had dug all day and then let his short-term results convince him that it was fruitless to pursue the goal—when in fact he was only a few spade fulls away from acres of diamonds. Many of us are in a similar situation when we fail to make the last few telephone calls that could change our life, when we don't do that little bit extra, go that little bit further that could have made all the difference. Persist until you achieve your goal—that way every goal will be forthcoming.

Learning: Excuses, distractions and fear are all a part of life. Acknowledge that they exist and look at how you can remove the existence of each one from your path. Recognise that these may be interferring with your current success plan and take immediate action to replace them with responsibility, focus and confidence going forward.

24 hours

The difference between people who achieve success and those who don't often boils down to how they spend their time. Those who succeed tend to do different things with their weekly allotted 168 hours than those who don't.

What's interesting about this is that all of us, if we put our minds to it, could achieve a lot more than we're achieving now. If you handle your time like most other successful people, you could achieve many times as much as you're achieving now. How? By getting organised. By working out what's important and what isn't.

A lot of people like to draw attention to themselves and win local fame by telling everyone how hard they work and how stressed they are. Feeling stressed shouldn't be anything to boast about. There's nothing heroic about feeling stressed. What's heroic is being able to pack a lot of things into your life and not feel under pressure. Successful people are able to do this. In fact, it's one of the main reasons why they're successful.

Getting organised is one of the keys to high achievement. But it's more than that: it's the *fundamental* of high achievement. It's identifying the things that need to be done and working out ways to fit them easily into your schedule. Once you get organised, you'll be amazed at how comfortably you get things done which would have seemed beyond you before.

It's a common misconception that the more you do during the day the more tired you are at the end of it. Tony Robbins once said that, 'It's not the things you do that tire you but the things you don't do'. I think this is very true. At the end of the day it's the six things you were supposed to do but failed to do, maybe because you procrastinated or just chose to avoid them, that really exhausted you mentally. But you won't feel mentally exhausted if you reach the end of the day, having completed everything on your 'to do' list, maybe failing to get the desired result in one or two cases but achieving great goals in others. If you've done all that, you may feel like relaxing but you'll also feel mentally charged.

As an example, here is how I spent one day recently, chosen at random from my diary. This kind of routine doesn't tire me. On the contrary, it energises me. It may seem a packed schedule, but I know I'm not operating to full capacity. I know I'll achieve more when I improve certain aspects of my systems and techniques.

MONDAY 14 MAY

Another day and the week is about to start. This is where you make the difference. It's what you make happen between sunrise and sunset that sets you apart.

5.15 a.m.: I get up every day at about this time. I find the best—perhaps only—time to get 30 minutes exercise in without distraction is before work. And as I choose to start work by 7.00 a.m. I need to get up at this time. I typically go to the gym in my apartment building for convenience, but I like to head down to Bondi Beach for an early-morning run and swim when I can.

6.30 a.m.: I drop by my favourite café on the way to work. It opens at 6.30 a.m. and I'm usually the first customer. I like to read through the newspapers and plan my day. Sometimes I meet with a member of my management team over coffee. I love the feel of getting a head start on my competitors. By the time I've exercised, read the papers and often met with my team, most of my competitors are still between the sheets.

I read the papers both to stay in touch with what's happening and also as a business development tool. I often tear out several articles that may provide business opportunities. Today I read that Starbucks Coffee Shops are coming to Australia. I want to make sure we're their agent to find them sites so I tear out the article to give to my Leasing Manager. From that action an important relationship may develop.

8.00 a.m.: Almost every week I lead our Sales Meeting. A time when all our sales team gets together to review the week, this is where we discuss new properties, recent sales and market trends. I always like to weave some coaching and motivation into that meeting. If I can spend 30–45 minutes a week to focus and fire up my main revenue earners, it's a great use of my time. Plus it keeps me very close to the coalface—to those in the sales trenches every day.

8.45 a.m.: My next regular meeting is with my Executive Assistant team. I have three Assistants who each have separate responsibilities. They are the world's best team of PAs and I wouldn't swap them for anyone. All young, passionate and customer focused. I run through my previous 24 hours with them. We look at each of my meetings and the key decisions and actions that came from them: what do I have to follow up and what's due from others? We also look ahead at the next 24 hours to see what the key meetings will be and how we can prepare. I usually like to channel my focus to one day at a time. I tend to pack so much in to a week that if I tried to keep focused on the week ahead, rather than just the next day, I'd get mentally tired. So all I have to do is be effective today; tomorrow will look after itself.

9.15 a.m.: Next I catch up with my Chief Operating Officer, Sheila Royles. She's a dynamo. I met Sheila when I was involved with the float of an Internet real estate company. She impressed me with her intelligence and energy, two key traits not often found in the same person. I also like her directness. She gets to the point and you know where you stand. We go through the week's outcomes and focus on our strategic goals for the future. We also use each other as a sounding board to work through challenges. Our conversations are always energetic, provocative and positive. No room for complaining or blaming; if we've got issues, we sort through them and move ahead.

10.00 a.m.: I meet with my Education and Special Events Manager. We have a big international real estate conference next week with over 1000 people coming from around the world. While we don't heavily advertise or brand the conference, it is funded and run entirely by our team. They have done a great job. Last year we had about 500 people and lost money, but this year it will be the best real estate conference in the world and we'll do well financially. Looking to the future, we see training and coaching as a great opportunity to develop other revenue streams, and it allows us to keep our own team exposed to the best trainers on the planet. We go through everything at the meeting, from the final layout of the room, speaker topics and even the music that will be played in the breaks. I really love to get involved in the detail. I have learned to delegate and get out of the way, but I also enjoy the opportunity to have a say on the detail nonetheless. Sometimes they listen.

10.45 a.m.: This meeting is about a new development in Brisbane that we're pitching for. I still love the thrill of the sale and the big pitch. This developer has secured the rights to work with Australian designer Marc Newson. It will be a winner. The site is good. The designer is hot. And I hope like hell we're selected to sell it. A major part of our pitch will be focused on our brand and the Internet. I know that the McGrath brand will work well with the developer's concept, I just need to make sure *they* know that.

12.10 p.m.: I'm meeting with a guy I've been trying to get to come and work for us. He's a great salesman and I know that with us he'd move up to a whole new level. But I know people are essentially conservative, afraid of making the wrong decisions, so I've got to reassure him that it'll work for him. The meeting went well and I sense he'll join us.

12.45 p.m.: I hate long lunches unless there's a worthwhile business agenda behind it. Then I see it as a business meeting with food. Today I'm ducking into No Names Restaurant. I've been going there since I was about 16—two decades years later nothing's changed. It's $6 for a bowl of spaghetti and $2 for a coffee downstairs. I usually get in and out in 30 minutes. On the way out I see my friend who owns an adjoining cafe. We're getting a home loan approved for his daughter so she can buy her first home with her boyfriend. My finance team told me the approval's through so I wanted to give them the good news. Now we've got to help them find a property.

1.45 p.m.: I don't take any incoming calls to the office unless it's either a VIP client, someone looking to sell a property or the property press. I get over 100 calls a day and if I took every one of them I'd never get anything done. So I have my team of assistants handle everything. They know exactly how I want things dealt with and do most of it without having to ask me. They give me a list of the calls I have to return about twice a day. I prefer email and tell most people I meet to email me as a preference. I return most of my telephone calls from the car between appointments. I take a quick 30 minutes out to return all my emails before my next meeting.

2.10 p.m.: My Marketing Manager drops by my office. He's concerned that I haven't signed off on the sales collateral for our new logo, but I'm not 100 per cent sure we've got it right yet. I run a lot of the business by intuition. Sometimes I don't know why but I have gut feelings about things. I have a philosophy about major decisions: if the answer within you isn't YES!, it's no. I'm going to take the designs up to my brother's place. He's a great sounding board, and so is his wife, Jodie. I'll watch how they react and I'll listen to what they say. I don't believe in spending thousands of dollars on research but I do believe in getting feedback from people I respect. It also gives me a great excuse to drive up and see one of my god-daughters, Anna (their gorgeous 12-month-old baby). I'll go there one night this week after work.

2.35 p.m.: I've got to fly, as I sometimes do a real estate segment on a TV show. We highlight a topical real estate story and do a quick 5-minute story, usually on-site somewhere. Today we're doing an interesting development that's fortunately right near the office. It's an old tobacco factory that's been converted into 10 warehouse apartments. One of my assistants does the research for me and puts down four or five key points on paper. I usually read it on the way to the shoot—sometimes I think it's best if the information's fresh. If I rehearsed or studied it too much it would affect the way I present it. When I get there the crew have already set up, as I'm 15 minutes late. The story goes really well. The studio asks me a few questions live as I walk the viewers through the apartment. Cameraman's happy. Producer's happy.

2.45 p.m.: Because I thought the filming would take longer I've got 45 minutes to my next appointment, so I hit my email. I get through about 30 to 45 emails an hour. They're often one- or two-word replies—rarely are they more than a paragraph. No spellchecks. Just fast communication.

3.30 p.m.: It's time for an important meeting I have each week with my Sales Managers. Sales are the lifeblood of the business, so this hour is one of the most critical. We've had a good month—in fact, we exceeded our stretch targets by about 30 per cent—but of course we've got to do it all again this month. So we have an agenda. Top of the agenda is top performers. I need to be aware of the high achievers so I can give them recognition. Poor performers and complaints are next on the agenda. I'd love to tell you we get no complaints—ever. But it's not the case. Our team provides exceptional service and the letters we get telling us this are incredible. However, we invariably get one or two complaints a week that must be addressed fast. If we do we'll win the client back and learn from the experience. If we don't, we'll lose the client. We discuss our Key Performance Indicators and look at any exceptions or variations. We track the number of calls we receive and make, and we telemarket almost every buyer and seller to check on our performance. The numbers are critical: they don't lie or tell half-truths. If our numbers are heading in the wrong direction it's time for massive action—today!

4.30 p.m.: This meeting is on the phone. I like to do as many meetings as possible on the phone because they're typically much faster than a face-to-face meeting. I need to run through some design changes for a small property development I'm involved in. It's my first-ever development and I've learnt so much during the process. We experienced hold-ups getting it out of council. My design brief to our architect, Ian Moore, was to design the most beautiful building he could for the site; a building that would inspire the residents. And he has. In fact, it's been nominated for an international architectural award. The new design works well, so we adjust the numbers on our feasibility. Whilst it must be beautiful it must also work financially or my partners won't want to do another. I enjoy juggling my own idealism with the pragmatic commercial world we live in. My project manager and I agree that we're on track and I ask him to provide my partners in the development with the new numbers. It's important to keep everyone in the loop.

5.30 p.m.: This is my last meeting of the day. I hate having meetings into the night. I like to 'go hard and go home', as Jim Cassidy said after winning the Melbourne Cup a few years ago. This meeting is to catch up with Kevin, the CEO of realestate.com.au. This is a public company that I have a fairly major stake in and I'm on the Board. It's my first public Board appointment and I love it. It's not much different from running your own business: you have a set of targets you have to meet; things get in the way and you've got to blast through them. Kevin and I meet as often as we can to go through sales issues. We're currently hiring a new National Sales Manager and I've found someone I think Kevin should meet. In fact, he's a friend of mine I hadn't seen for a while until I ran into him on a plane a few days ago. He told me he was going for a new position and I suggested he talk to us. The meeting went well and it looks like he'll be offered the position, subject to Board ratification. I think he'll be terrific—just what we need. And in this nanosecond world of the Internet you can't afford to miss an opportunity.

7.15 p.m.: I'm over for the day. I was hoping to catch a movie but the last meeting went a little longer than I'd planned. So I'm heading off home for a quick meal. I never eat after 7.30 and I try not to eat a heavy meal in the evening. So I'll have a bowl of pasta and steamed vegetables as soon as I get home. I call one of my godchildren on the way home to see how her day was.

Looking back, it was a very productive day. Sometimes you get on a roll—get into the zone and things turn out right. Today was a good one. I haven't had time to prepare for tomorrow, so I'll do it in the morning. I'll be in bed by 9.30 and asleep by 10.

Learning: You can fit a lot more into your day than you think. Don't be afraid to fill your life with exciting, productive and challenging appointments and events. Make sure each one has a purpose and a goal—preferably one that can change your life.

PART 3

Staying Successful

Inspiration is all around us

Many people believe that knowledge is the key to success in business and in other fields. In one sense it is, yet on its own knowledge is useless. In fact it's the implementation of knowledge that holds the key. And to implement knowledge the key is inspiration.

Inspiration is what gets the adrenalin flowing. It's what releases the energy that enables you to fight through a tough period. It's the spark that triggers the explosion of effort that you need to lift yourself to a new level. The question is: how and where do we find it and how do we keep it?

As an early riser I normally turn in by 9.30 p.m.,

but I stayed up late one night to watch Mark Philippoussis win a marathon five-setter in the Australian Open tennis tournament which dragged on until about 11.30 p.m. Next morning the match was featured on a morning television show that I happened to watch before leaving for work so I could see the highlights of the game. To my amazement, the presenter crossed live to the tournament centre, and there at 7 o'clock in the morning was Philippoussis working at his ground shots on the practice court.

I'd admired him the previous night for his skill, his athleticism, his fighting spirit. But I admired him much more for what I saw him doing now. Here was a guy who, by the time he'd done his press conference and made his way back to the hotel, probably hadn't made it to bed until 1.30 a.m. that morning. Yet at 7 a.m. he was back on the practice court, trying to perfect his game.

I found this inspiring. No matter how successful you may be, you have to keep practising, keep improving your game, keep checking to make sure you're headed in the right direction. Like Philippoussis, you need to assess your game constantly.

If your game has a flaw—if you're not good with people, say, or if you're not organised—work at eliminating the flaw. If you know people who succeed where you fail, watch them closely. See how they do what they do. If you know people who are highly motivated, talk to them about it. What motivates them? If they go through a soft spot, how do they reinvigorate themselves to get going again?

Failure is a precursor to success, but when the inevitable failure comes along, can you stop it affecting you? Personally, I haven't found a way to do so. The question, then, having come up against failure, is how do you find a way out of the situation?

If we were to look around, we would see a lot of people in all walks of life who are doing things that have the capacity to inspire us. The trouble is we often have blinkers on and don't see them. We don't look beyond our own world, the one we've been brought up in and are familiar with, the one we've drawn all our experience from, the one that has created the way we think. There must have been several hundred thousand viewers who saw Philippoussis on TV that morning, but maybe only a handful saw the inspiration in what he was doing.

What we need to do is actively look for the inspiration every day, whether in books, tapes, on television, the Internet, or maybe in the person sitting across the coffee table from you. Almost everything around us has the potential to inspire you if you're seeking inspiration, but little will inspire you if you're not.

Some people have a special talent for inspiring others. Businessman Rodney Adler, a friend of mine, is one of these. Rodney is a great people person: he has a gift for getting people enthused with what he has in mind and for inspiring them to lift themselves to a higher level of performance to accomplish it. He can do in the business environment what a football coach does at half-time with his players: he can get them to lift their game when extra effort and intensity are needed.

Yet you don't necessarily need to meet someone like Rodney Adler to become inspired and stay that way. Many people you meet can inspire you if you're on the lookout for inspiration. Often my most junior staff inspire me. I've had people who have been out of work for six months, and rejected for many positions, knock on the door for a job—that inspires me.

INSPIRATION IS ALL AROUND US

So look for inspiration everywhere. Make a habit of seeking it out. Then, suddenly, you'll find that becoming successful and staying that way isn't as hard as you might think.

Conducting a personal audit

Each year most businesses have an audit done of their financial accounts. The purpose of the audit is to check that things are as they should be, and if they're not, it helps identify problems to get them on track. Similarly, most people get an annual check-up done on their car by getting a mechanic to examine the engine, tyres and body to make sure that there are no faults. But the most important asset you'll ever own can go for years without an audit or review—that is, of course, *you*. So I'm going to suggest that you take a few minutes now and look at the key areas of your life. Look at them to test they're functioning at peak performance because if you need a tune-up now's a great time to do it.

THE BIG ROCKS

First look at things like health and fitness, personal relationships, peace of mind, personal development, career and finances. These are some of the 'big rock' categories you'd want to have tracking well. Take a moment to rate yourself in these areas between 0–10—a score of 10 being perfection—to see how you'd score yourself. Be honest. In fact, brutally honest. This is an opportunity to discover where you're performing well and where you need to improve.

Once you've rated yourself in these areas, take a look at the results. Circle anything you rated less than an 8 out of 10. For some, there could be one big circle! It can be surprising and scary to see that some of the most important areas in your life may only be rating at 4 or 5 out of 10.

The next and more important task is to write down next to each area what it would take to move towards a 10. For example, if you're a cigarette smoker and rated yourself 4 out of 10 for health and fitness, giving up smoking would probably take you to an immediate 7. You might also jot down '30 minutes exercise a day' alongside it, and when that's in place you might rate yourself at 8. So two simple actions or commitments could double the quality of your health and fitness.

This is a simple but potent exercise that should ideally be performed several times a year.

EVALUATING YOUR HABITS

Moving on from the big rock categories, let's drill down into some of your important day-to-day habits. In seminars, I usually get people in the audience to evaluate themselves. I invite them to write down ten things that they consider vital in achieving success. They might be things like attitude, time management, goal setting, focus and so on.

Next time you're tempted to blame some external circumstance for your lack of success, work out why you've rated yourself only 5 out of 10 for time management, and decide how long you're going to accept that as part of your life. Or say you gave yourself a 6 out of 10 for attitude. Attitude is probably the most important thing in the world, and you've rated yourself only 6 out of 10. When are you going to change that?

Here is the crucial thing: don't simply rely on your own evaluation of yourself. Ask two or three close friends or colleagues to do an audit on you, too. Ask them to rate you from 0 to 10, honestly and without regard to your feelings, in matters like:

- personal presentation
- attitude
- self-management
- personality
- persistence and resilience
- honesty
- health and fitness
- ability to delegate
- communication skills (including the ability to listen)
- taking action

It doesn't matter who you ask to do this so long as they know you well and are prepared to be completely honest. It could be your spouse, your children, your boss, your PA, your best friend. If there's only one qualified person willing to do it, that's fine. Two or three is ideal, but one is enough.

Any score below 8 needs to be addressed. Go to the people who assessed you and ask them to explain why they rated you at that level. As before, ask them to be very honest. This type of feedback is critical. It's the only way you can form an accurate picture of yourself.

Don't stop there. Having focused on the areas of life where you seem to be letting yourself down (usually, these can be narrowed down to two or three), try to find people you've heard of who are particularly strong in these areas. Let's imagine you've been judged to lack persistence. You may be lucky enough to know someone personally who has achieved great things through persistence, in which case speak to that person directly. Or you could search your library or the Internet for people who have shown great strength in this area and try to find clues in their stories as to how you can follow their examples and improve in that area.

A great way to improve your thinking is to have people challenge your ideas and thoughts. This is one of the main reasons why so many prominent business people employ business coaches or mentors. It's the same as having a personal fitness trainer. A personal trainer pushes us to our physical limits. When we attempt to get fit on our own, we tend to become a little lazy and take shortcuts. But when we're working with someone else who has high standards and is focused on us, we invariably push ourselves to our limits. Mentally, it's exactly the same. Being grilled and asked tough questions pushes our thinking to a new level.

IF MICHAEL JOHNSON HAS A COACH, WHY NOT YOU?

Why does a top athlete like Michael Johnson need a coach? If he's as good as he is, if he already knows so much about the technique of sprinting, what can a coach possibly teach him? The simple answer is that Michael Johnson is incapable of judging for himself if what he is doing is right or wrong. He needs a coach to look objectively at what he is doing, to identify faults and suggest ways he can improve. In fact, he probably has several coaches: an athletics coach, a mental coach and a nutritionist.

Now if Johnson and all the other top athletes in the world use coaches, shouldn't the rest of us have them, too? The answer is yes. I've used coaches most of the time I've been in business. I rely on them to give me honest opinions, to provide objective feedback, to offer informed input on how I can improve my performance.

As I write this I have two business coaches. They operate at different levels. One of them (I call him my life coach) teaches me how to improve mentally and emotionally. I meet with him every three months. The other coach provides me with feedback on how I'm performing in day-to-day business operations. I meet with him every week. We sit down and he holds me accountable for what I've done or not done since our last meeting. We review the goals I'd set for myself then check how many I've managed to achieve, examine why the other goals weren't achieved, consider whether the goals themselves need changing, and look at how I plan to achieve future goals.

This kind of coaching is becoming popular among business people. Quite a few chief executives of big public companies in Australia employ 'mentors' to review their performance and act as sounding boards. Maybe some people are able to ask themselves the tough questions and give themselves truthful, accurate answers, but most of us benefit from someone else to challenge us.

MAKE THE MOST OF YOUR NETWORK

Your coach doesn't have to be a professional who charges a fee. He or she just has to be a caring person who is close to you and whose opinion you respect. It could be a peer partner. By peer partner I mean someone from your social peer group (friends, relatives) or business peer group (work colleagues) who you're accessible to, who you feel comfortable with, who you're happy to reveal your private thoughts to and who you're prepared to become a partner with in this exercise on an ongoing basis. You can make it a reciprocal arrangement. The important thing is to schedule regular meetings. Arrange to meet every week or fortnight for coffee and exchange views on how each of you has performed.

Why do I suggest regular meetings? Because if,

day after day, you let things drift for too long they'll get away from you completely. We all need regular review points that we can put in our diary and adhere to. We need to be challenged at fixed intervals with questions about our performance: Are you on track? What's going right? What's going wrong? What do you need to start doing? What do you need to stop doing? What's working that you need to continue doing? Some people are lucky enough to work for companies that review their performance regularly and provide them with feedback. But most companies don't do this, so people have to organise review points of their own.

There is another advantage in meeting regularly with a peer partner to exchange assessments of how you're both performing: it forces you to articulate the issue you're dealing with. We all tend to live inside our heads too much, which causes us confusion. When an issue is merely running around in your head, it cannot have much syntax. When, on the other hand, you are required to talk about it to someone else, you have to put the issue in some type of order and focus on its key elements. The mere process of doing this enables you to clear the issue up.

As we all know, fixing someone else's problem is always a lot easier than fixing our own. Why? Because you can view other people's problems objectively and with perspective. You can see at once where the errors are. When the errors are part of your life, though, it's almost impossible to see them with the same clarity.

CONFRONT THE REALITY OF YOURSELF

I spoke earlier of the need for personal evaluation before you start setting goals for yourself. I suggested you ask someone close to you, whether your spouse, your children, your boss, your PA or your best friend, to mark you with brutal honesty on a scale of zero to ten on how you rate in key areas of your life. You can do exactly the same thing at review meetings. Ask the other person to rate you, on things such as attitude, efficiency, personality, appearance. And do the same for your peer partner.

Naturally, you must insist on complete mutual honesty. The exercise is pointless otherwise. You can expect a degree of pain in hearing the truth, but it is pain which leads to improvement. Of course, what your peer partner says may not always be totally accurate—it's just their opinion, after all—but you still should hear it. And, not everything you hear will be painful. You'll also be told what you're doing right, so you can take pleasure and pride in that. If you keep doing things right but never have that success acknowledged in some way, subconsciously you begin to wonder if there's any point in achieving more success. So celebration of success is also important.

It may help to see the exchange you have with your peer partner or coach, and the subsequent changes you intend to make, as a detoxification. You're getting rid of the things that are polluting your life. These could be bad habits, or an unhealthy diet, or friends who are holding you back. The latter—negative friends—can be problematic to some people. Cutting off friends or acquaintances may seem drastic, but your life is far too important to spend the rest of it socialising with someone who is a negative influence. The alternative is to speak to them about it. Tell them that you're trying to improve your attitude, that you know that every time you get together you tend to complain about this or that and you want to cut it out. Suggest that you make a pact together never to talk negatively about anyone, that you try it for three days to see how it works—or that if either one of you does talk negatively a $5 penalty results.

Success is making the best of who you are. We are who we are, and none of us should want to be anyone else. We should all desire, however, to be the best that we can be. One of my mentors when I started in real estate was a very successful agent named Andrew Gibbons. For me, he was an icon, a model to emulate. I came to know that one of Andrew's great strengths was his networking ability. You'd see him in almost every Sunday newspaper—at a cocktail party, speaking at a conference, opening an exhibition. I wanted to emulate Andrew's success in real estate, but I wondered if I could ever match his amazing ability to network.

I thought hard about it and decided I wouldn't change who I was. There was no way I would want to become a great networker or a socialite, even if it helped make me successful. So I decided I would compensate for my lack of natural networking flair and social skills by doing other things better. I resolved to work harder than anyone else and maintain a 100 per cent focus.

So I didn't try to become another Andrew Gibbons, and I've no doubt now that that was the right choice. We all can achieve success or even greatness being just who we are.

Perfect health

There are some success-oriented people I know who would come to this chapter, see the heading and skip it, believing that health has little to do with achieving and maintaining success. In fact, I believe it is has everything to do with it. Surely your health must be the number one priority on your success hierarchy? What's the point of achieving in other areas of life if your health ends up suffering in the process?

Health is a big issue—perhaps the biggest, and

it's one on which the statistics are pretty telling. Here are some shocking truths about our population.

- 7.4 million Australians (56 per cent) are seriously overweight.
- 40.6 million drug prescriptions were dispensed for cardiovascular drugs in the last 12 months.
- For a 40-year-old male, the current risk of having coronary disease is 1:2—that means the average male only has a 50/50 chance of *not* having coronary disease.
- 41 per cent of all deaths result from cardiovascular disease.

Frightening facts, but fortunately, there are three simple keys to not becoming a statistic and being healthy. They are diet, exercise and sleep.

We know that energy and enthusiasm are two critical elements in the achievement of goals. Both of these are very hard to produce whilst in a state of poor health. Yet many people seem to have accepted that ill-health or even serious illness is inevitable. There are four or five simple habits that will not only ward off disease and illness but, if you practice them regularly, will put you in the top few percent of the population for health.

QUALITY ENERGY

What you eat and drink is an all-important factor. It largely determines whether you're healthy or not. As someone once said, 'Most people are digging their graves with their teeth.'

Although it's hard to avoid using it, I actually don't like the word 'diet'. It has unfortunate connotations, most of which have to do with the weight-loss eating regimens you see in popular magazines. I prefer the term 'food management'. If you can manage your money and your investments you should be able to manage what you eat, which really means adopting healthy eating habits.

Food is the energy that drives our magnificent machines. And just like a formula-one team would never consider placing anything other than the highest-grade fuel in their car's tank, neither should we compromise the quality of the fuel we put in our bodies. In fact, when you look at the diet of the average person—laden with preservatives, toxins and processed ingredients—it's hardly surprising that bowel cancer is one of the great killers of our society.

And in an age where, for the average person, quality food choices abound wherever you go, there is no excuse for our poor eating habits. In fact, the word 'habit' is the clue to this puzzle, as it has been throughout this book. Create excellent eating habits, put your body on cruise control and it'll be effortless.

You have a much better chance of changing your eating habits if you're level-headed and practical about it. In the first place, you need to persevere with the eating program you decide to follow, so the program must be sensible. Attempt only what you know you can do, and then make sure you keep doing it. If you swear off coffee or chocolate for life, you probably won't stick to it for more than a few weeks. You'll feel you've failed and you may be tempted to give up the program altogether. Sure, you can do strict diets in short-term bursts. I often do 30-day cleansing diets in which things like coffee and chocolate are off limits, but I'd never attempt to impose a regimen like that on myself permanently. Whatever you take on has to be a long-term health-maintenance program that you can stick to.

Attitude is as important in maintaining good eating habits as it is in every other area of our lives. Have a positive attitude to your healthy eating program you're about to adopt. Don't focus on the things you can't eat—the junk food, the fat foods. If you do, they'll be the things you crave. Focus on the all the good things you can eat—the refreshing salads, the tasty vegetables, the delicious fruit and fresh seafood. Let people close to you know what you're doing. Share your commitment to good eating with the people you have breakfast or lunch with. Take the list of foods you can eat to your regular café or restaurant and ask the chef not to deviate from the list when you come to eat there. Ask for their support. Make it a fun thing and get them involved.

Don't worry if you can't see the food you want to eat on the restaurant menu. When I go to a restaurant, I rarely even look at the menu. I'll simply ask the waiter to put together, say, a pasta with a salad or some steamed vegetables. Maybe some fettuccine with a fresh salad of avocado, tomato and lettuce. It may not be on the menu, but virtually every restaurant I've ever been to, whether cheap or expensive, will prepare a meal like this on request.

My own diet isn't nutritionally perfect. I usually have one coffee a day. I occasionally eat a bar of chocolate. About once a week I love a bowl of ice-cream.

It doesn't matter. The important thing, and the key to the whole subject of good nutrition, is that most of what I eat is good-quality, fresh food. This is the basic rule of practical healthy eating: treating yourself to the odd *bad* thing is okay provided that most of what you eat—say, 80 per cent—is good.

Also, if you regularly put good food inside you, there won't be much room left for anything bad. Eat a few pieces of fruit for breakfast, for instance, and you won't feel like a plate of sausages and eggs.

Here are the basics of my own daily eating routine. I don't say you need to follow this routine in particular, but it can be a useful guide for those who don't have a plan in mind. It has certainly worked for me.

BREAKFAST

Three pieces of fresh fruit (not out of a tin). This sets me up for the day with lots of fibre, minerals and vitamins. A glass of freshly squeezed juice. (I make the juice in a blender from fresh fruit or vegetables. Carrot and ginger juice is great.) A cup of coffee. I drink this at a café on the way to work each morning while I scan the morning newspapers. Coffee isn't good for you, but one cup a day won't kill you either.

LUNCH

A plate of fresh salad or a bowl of steamed vegetables, with either a grilled piece of fish or chicken breast. Provided you have either salad or vegetables, it doesn't matter so much what else you eat it with it. Eat a meat pie with the bowl of vegetables and you're probably doing okay. Eat a meat pie *without* the vegetables and you could be doing yourself harm. Again, it's a case of focusing on the good things, knowing that if a few bad things work their way into your diet your body will cope.

DINNER

The same as lunch: a plate of fresh salad or a bowl of steamed vegetables. Whichever one I eat at lunch,

I try to eat the other at dinner. Again, I don't worry too much what I eat it with so long as the salad or vegetables are the main part of the meal. Grilled seafood is great. Japanese food is also healthy and tasty.

If you can start doing all this tomorrow—have fresh fruit and a freshly squeezed juice for breakfast, a salad or a bowl of steamed vegetables for lunch or dinner, and a good vitamin and mineral supplement—you'll be giving yourself a rock-solid foundation for good health. You'll be taking in enough good things for your body to get back into balance.

If you suddenly crave a Mars bar it's because your body is out of balance. Will you still crave a Mars bar once you get your body back into balance? Occasionally, but most of the time you won't.

Here are a few more habits that will look after you for life:

Eat only until you're two-thirds full
Most people eat too much. Perhaps forced from childhood to 'finish everything on your plate', we develop habits of overeating. And today there is the

constant barrage of social and business lunches, each consisting of several courses, which are hard to avoid. With every lunch and dinner have a serving of fruit or vegetables. The first thing I look at when I sit down to look at a lunch or dinner menu is the salad options. I make sure that before I eat anything else I have a bowl of fresh salad or vegetables. If they're not on the menu just ask. With regard to fruit I make sure that every day I eat at least three pieces in the morning.

Cut down or eliminate alcohol
Alcohol creeps up on most people, as it is one of the 'socially accepted' toxins or drugs in our society. Yet if someone today were to invent a substance or liquid that had the effect of totally changing your personality, where extended use often caused disease of the liver and resulted in an alarming per cent of all deaths, it would never be approved by the authorities.

I have never drunk alcohol, a fortunate spin-off from my early sports career—and also, no doubt, a result from my father's untimely death at the hands of alcohol. You may not want to or even need to eliminate alcohol from your diet, but look at reducing your intake and frequency. Perhaps limit the days you drink alcohol: only drink on Tuesdays, Fridays and Saturdays, say. And have the sense to stop before you get intoxicated. The word intoxicated actually means 'taking in toxins'—think about it!

Drink at least two litres of spring water daily
Our body is mostly water. It loves water. And the process of constant detoxification—a sort of daily spring clean of your system—is greatly enhanced by regular intakes of water.

Don't smoke
You cannot be intelligent and smoke. This is not one to reduce, it's definitely one to eliminate.

Don't use drugs
I hate drugs. They're one of the saddest parts of our society, in my opinion. Unfortunately, some people have been deluded into thinking there are 'recreational' or 'social' drugs and 'bad' drugs. All drugs are bad. Full stop. So be very careful about

any propaganda that might have you thinking there are varying degrees of acceptability in taking drugs.

Avoid highly processed food and sugar-rich food

I eat white bread. I like the taste and because I look after most other areas of my diet, I can probably eat it without any negative side effects. But I urge you to predominantly eat 'live food' rather than canned, processed and preserved foods. For example, I never eat anything from a tin. I know that they've had to add lots of chemicals to it back at the canning plant in order to get it to the table. I also don't drink soft drink. It's loaded with sugar and chemicals big time. And by the way, the taste of a freshly squeezed juice outdoes canned drink by a mile. You just need to get organised and either buy yourself a juicer or track down a good shop that makes fresh juice.

Invest 2 per cent of your time into getting and staying fit

You have 168 hours at your disposal every week. You need only invest about three of these hours into getting or keeping fit. A tiny 30 minutes a day, 6 days a week will have you in good shape. And it can be great fun in the process.

Remember when you were a kid. Most of the day was spent tearing around the playground, park or house burning up inordinate amounts of energy. Then, as we came under the scrutiny of the small poppies around us, we were told not to behave with as much zest and energy—to sit down and watch 'Play School', perhaps. And what often grew from that was a sedentary lifestyle.

So the first step is to get the energy back into your life. Be active. For example, I rarely take elevators. I'm not scared of them, but if I'm going somewhere and it's on the first five levels of a building, I'll take the stairs. It's great exercise and keeps me moving. I also love playing touch football. It's not exercise to me; it's a game that gives me incredible enjoyment and simultaneously works out my muscles.

I suggest you look to developing a morning ritual, a 20–40 minute routine that you can undertake at the beginning of each day. There are a few good reasons to exercise at the beginning of the day as opposed to the end. The first one is that it gets done. Really. How many times have you had every positive intention of exercising at the end of the day and either a late appointment or a more exciting alternative pops into your schedule? Learn from the realities of life. Adjust your routine so you make the things happen that are important. I exercise at 5.15 a.m. each morning. I'm finished by 6.00 a.m., then showered and dressed by 6.30 and into the day before most people are even awake. It gives me an incredible start and I know that an important part of my life has been looked after again. That's part of the second reason I suggest morning exercise. It gives you a mental edge. It keeps you sharp and you feel fantastic all day.

I'm not one to suggest that you need to exercise to the point of pain to receive benefit. Quite the opposite. Once exercise goes beyond the point of pleasure I believe it starts to wear your body down, and the associated stress negates much of the benefits derived from the activity. So look at things you enjoy and don't overdo them. If you like running, great. Run until you feel you've had enough. The same goes for walking, dancing, bike riding, roller blading, yoga or whatever turns you on. Just do it.

SLEEP: THE TIME TO RECHARGE

The mistake most of us make about sleep is to underestimate the importance of it. Many consider it a time-wasting activity that ought to be kept to a minimum. For many people, 'minimum' means about five hours' sleep a night. I'm as busy as anyone, yet I make sure I sleep at least seven and preferably eight hours every night. I go very hard during the twelve hours I work each day, and the reason I'm able to do this is that I allow my body to recover, both physically and mentally, with sleep.

Many people go hard at night as well as during the day and then wonder why their body isn't functioning well or breaks down on them. Your car wouldn't function well, either, if you drove it 19 hours a day and didn't keep it in tune.

Sleep is the big opportunity the body has each day to repair and replenish itself. I believe it is so important that we should try to enhance the quality any way we can. I have a special routine to make sure I sleep well. I have a hot shower before going to bed, put lavender in an oil burner near my bed, black out the room completely and relax into a deep sleep. Work out your own routine, but recognise that this is a key area of health—so don't sweep it under the carpet.

ABSENCE OF STRESS EQUALS PEACE OF MIND

Throughout this book I use the term 'stress' to describe a feeling that most people experience with some frequency. I don't go along with the idea that stress is a condition as such; it's really your response to certain external stimuli. Exams are an example. Some people thrive on exams whereas others fall apart. Football grand finals are another example. Some people play their best game of the season in the grand final, others play their worst. It all depends on how you choose to respond to a particular occasion.

The important thing to recognise is that stress isn't an external force that we're powerless to resist. Stress does exist, but it exists only when we let it. This being the case, it follows that we ought to be able to eliminate stress by making changes to our mind-set. What those changes are depends, of course, on what's causing the stress.

Some people say that real estate is a very stressful business. I tell my sales team that stress in our business invariably results from not doing the right things before the stress. If you've got a work routine and you follow it conscientiously—if you ring your clients every day, you turn up on time for your appointments, you follow through, you get submissions in on time and so on—real estate isn't a stressful job, it's just fun.

The same thing can be said about other jobs that are supposedly stressful. Whatever business you're in, if a customer is on the phone screaming at you it's often because you didn't process their order correctly, you didn't get back to them with information or you slipped up in some other way. And even if their anger is totally unreasonable you can still choose not to allow the incident to create stress for you. It's a choice.

It's also vital that we act to reduce or eliminate stress from our lives, because feeling stressed is harmful to your health. Consult a natural health practitioner about a health problem, and one of the first things he or she will ask you is whether you're feeling stress in your life. If you are, you'll be advised to eliminate the cause of it, because there's every chance that the stress is the root cause of your illness. The American doctor, Norman Cousins did a lot to pioneer the idea that our mental state affects our physical state. Stricken with a debilitating disease himself, Cousins discovered that laughter relieved his symptoms. By doing so, he put his finger on the nature of stress. It's impossible to feel stressed while you're laughing.

Stress also has a negative influence on how we perform in our daily lives. Stress tenses us up, and when we're tense it's impossible to perform at peak levels. Look at the fastest athletes in the world, people like Michael Johnson, and you'll see that when they run they're in a relaxed state. It's also a fact that Michael Johnson constantly stretches himself to higher levels. He has an intense will to win. But he doesn't stretch himself to the point where his will to win turns into stress. This is the zone we should all try to operate in: a zone where we're stretched but still relaxed. This is where peak performance is achieved.

If there's stress in your life, identify it. Begin by writing down all the things in your week that you dread, all the things that make you feel uncomfortable. Then, one by one, try to work out how you can either eliminate them altogether or change your attitude to them so they're no longer stressful.

Another common cause of work-related stress is a person's relationship with his or her boss. I initially disliked my first boss in real estate, and the reason was that he used to hold me accountable. I'd come in to work and he'd ask me whether I'd done the four things he'd asked me to do the day before. Generally I'd done only two of them, so he'd come down hard on me and I'd feel stressed. Eventually, I recognised that the stress wasn't coming from him: it was coming from me not doing what I was supposed to do. So I started doing everything I was asked to do and more, and from then on our relationship changed. The stress disappeared and my old boss has since become one of my closest friends.

Absence of stress equals peace of mind, and peace of mind is something I regard as an essential characteristic of successful people. People who spend their lives agonising over problems or feeling stressed out can hardly consider themselves successful, no matter how much money they make. We may not be able to avoid stress altogether as the everyday challenges of life that we all have to deal with stretch us to some extent. But stress and worry must not be allowed to dominate our lives.

Learning: Your health is the most precious asset you have. Quality food, moderate exercise and restful sleep are all you need to maintain yourself in peak condition.

Nice guys and girls *don't* finish last

We all know the saying that 'nice guys finish last'. Many people believe it's true. Maybe it is sometimes, but in today's business world it's honesty that counts.

People who reach the top and stay there are typically people of integrity who care about their staff, their customers and their investors. It doesn't mean they can't be tough, but it does mean they're not ruthless. What I call ruthless is getting rid of two or three staff because your bonus is based on profitability and you want to get a bigger bonus. I see tough as making decisions that are right and fair for everyone concerned, even if they do cause short-term pain.

There are many examples of business people who are honest and decent people that have made it to the top. Peter Ritchie, who used to head up McDonald's in Australia, is one who comes to mind. He has been one of the nation's most successful business people in recent years, yet he's also one of the nicest people I've ever met. It's the Peter Ritchies of the world who we ought to focus on and use as role models. Sure, there are some people in business who rip others off and make money in the process. But people of this type are rare, and in any case they don't last very long. In fact, I would argue that unless you're essentially decent and honest it's virtually impossible to achieve long-term success in business.

INTEGRITY EQUALS SUCCESS

I was asked at a seminar recently what personal qualities people responded to most in business. My reply was honesty and integrity. I am totally convinced of this. What people want more than anything in business is straight dealing and straight talking. Yet straight talking isn't common at all levels of business and, in particular, it isn't common in my business. People like to bend the truth, sugar-coat the truth or conceal it. Sometimes they do it so well that they get away with it, but more often than not the people they're dealing with are awake to it.

People respond so well to honesty. I discovered this soon after I began selling real estate. I came to realise that what the customer really wants is a straight deal. All I had to do is be honest with customers and follow them up—nothing hard about that. I made a point of telling prospective buyers about the shortcomings of any property first-up. Invariably, they reacted favourably, probably because they found the honesty refreshing.

If I was selling a house, I would tell the buyer that there were a few problems with the house that I thought they should know about. If a couple were close to making an offer for a house I was showing them, I'd say, 'Before you decide to buy, there are a few things I'd like you to see.' Then I'd pull the couch out and show them a patch of rising damp in the wall. They would ask if this was a major problem, and I'd say not really: I'd already obtained a quote from a builder who could fix it for $500. This wasn't a big cost in relation to the purchase of the house, so they would probably say they could live with that. Then I'd take them out the back, put up a ladder and invite them to have a look at a lean-to roof which had a bit of rust. I'd tell them, 'In four or five years' time you're going to need some money set aside for replacing this, so I'd like you to be aware of it.'

People responded incredibly well. They'd buy the property, love me for being so up-front with them, and usually refer everyone they knew to me because they'd found someone who would give them a straight deal. Honesty, even brutal honesty, rarely ruins a sale. In fact, it nearly always consolidates the sale.

Consider the case I've just described. People usually find out the faults in the property themselves. They call in an architect who discovers the rising damp and the rust in the roof. When this happens and you haven't told them about it, they feel doubtful about everything else you've told them about the property, even though what you've said may be true.

GETTING PERSONAL

Some time ago one of our business leaders was quoted as saying that he never allows personal relationships to influence any business decision. I regard this as an outdated concept. The world is changing. Today, it's impossible to draw a hard and fast line between the personal and the impersonal in business. Increasingly, people are coming to recognise that an intuitive and personal approach in management works best.

You need to build good personal relationships with your customers, and you need to build good personal relationships with your team. Every day at 10 a.m. I walk around the office so I can get to see as many of my team as I can and check on how they're going. This is called 'Management By Walking Around'. I do it because I recognise, as a CEO, that it is important for me to be in touch with all parts of my business and for all my team to have access to me on a regular basis.

I had personal relationships in mind when I referred earlier to Peter Ritchie of McDonald's. As I observed him, I realised that the secret of Ritchie's success in business was that he was a great people person. He understood that to achieve great results he needed to enrol other people in his vision. He had a gift for nurturing people, whether they were his managers, franchisees, customers or clients. He encouraged and recognised achievement and he saluted it when it happened, and in the process he lifted people around him to higher levels. He is, undoubtedly, a nice guy who finished first.

Personal marketing is frequently the difference between success and mediocrity, especially in people-related work. Look around any big office. You'll find some people earning award rates and some earning two or three times as much. Why is this? One possible reason is that the better-paid people are more skilled or experienced. But in almost every case you'll also find that the top earners have marketed themselves better within the company.

Why does one fruiterer in a suburban shopping centre prosper and another fail? Is it because one of them has better fruit or cheaper fruit? Maybe, but it's more likely to be because of the way the successful fruiterer displays his fruit, speaks to customers, and smiles when he gives them their change. This is all personal marketing.

Don't feel hesitant about pushing yourself forward, about marketing yourself and your business, about trying to advance yourself as far as you can go. Many people don't feel comfortable with this strategy. They don't want to seem too pushy. But look at it this way: only by looking after yourself, by advancing your own interests, can you get to a position where you can materially help others. It's a bit like being in an emergency on a plane: when the oxygen masks drop, unless you grab your own mask and use it you won't be able to help anyone else. The people who are best able to help and support their community are the people who have been successful in their own lives.

I suggest you promote yourself as hard as you can, knowing that you can preserve your decency, honesty and relationships at the same time. How do you go about promoting yourself? The first thing to do is work out a personal marketing strategy. Let me tell you of my own experience.

When I began my first real estate firm, I was largely unknown in the business and had only a few contacts. I didn't have much money to spend on advertising and I had almost no profile. So when I came to create a personal marketing strategy, I had to create it out of nothing. My strategy, simply, was to offer better service than any real estate agent in the world had ever offered before. My aim was to provide customers with such fantastic service that after they left me they'd be tempted to say to everyone they met that day, 'I've just had the best *service* experience of my life.'

This strategy wasn't really hard to work out, because it's pretty obvious what customers want. They want a straight deal, quality information, and they want you to listen, care and be attentive.

Watch some real estate agents going into a sales presentation and you'll see dollar signs flashing in their eyeballs. They're focusing on how much commission they're going to make if the sale goes through. The customer can sense this. When I worked in sales I never knew how much I'd make out of a sale. I knew that if I did this, if I had it in my head that I stood to make $10 000 if I sold Bill's house and only $3000 if I sold another, I might have let that influence me.

The strategy worked. People loved the service, they talked about it, other people heard it and talked about it, and soon a network of contacts began to develop.

The point of this is that you don't need to have a high profile to market yourself successfully. You don't need a public relations consultant sending out press releases about you and setting up interviews with magazines and television.

Let's imagine you're a retail assistant in a department store. Your personal marketing strategy might be to brighten the day of everyone who comes to your counter by dealing with people cheerfully and honestly. If you did this, it wouldn't be long before your excellent service was recognised both inside and outside the store, and once you gained this kind of recognition all types of opportunities would present themselves.

A few years ago a television reporter who was a friend of mine decided to sell a property in East Sydney. She contacted me and I spoke to her about the sale, but I sensed that for some reason she was reluctant to let me handle it. This surprised me, because apart from the fact that we had a business relationship, I was sure our sales strategy was the right one and that we could do a better job than anyone else. Tracey did give me the business eventually, but I remained curious about her initial hesitation. I asked her about it. She told me she'd met a young real estate agent not long down from the country, who was working for a small firm in Elizabeth Bay. He'd impressed her with his personal manner, honesty and reliability and he'd given her such marvellous service, she said, that she was tempted to go with him.

I made a note of his name, and after we sold Tracey's property I phoned him and invited him to join me for a cup of coffee. Later, I offered him a job. Today, at twenty-four years of age, he is one of the top salesmen in my company and is among the top ten in Australia. Some of this can be traced to the fact that, whether he realised it or not, he had a great personal marketing strategy. His strategy was to give outstanding service: return calls, behave pleasantly, turn up on time, follow up, answer questions honestly, and to do everything else he promised to do. Tracey was impressed by it, I got to hear about it and a new opportunity for this young salesman opened up. This flow-on effect is always on the cards when someone provides wonderful service.

Marketing yourself is essential, no matter how reluctant you may feel about doing it. It doesn't have to be an up-front, chest-thumping exercise. It can be done in subtle ways. Personal presentation is one of them. Just presenting yourself better when you go to work each day will have an impact, because whether you like it or not, people do form an impression of you before you open your mouth.

A friend of mine, a rock musician, has a tattoo on his forearm. I make no judgment about tattoos personally, but not everyone likes them. He used to turn up for job interviews wearing short-sleeved shirts, and he couldn't understand why no employer would take him on. I suggested to him one day that his tattoos might have something to do with it. I said that many people had preconceptions about people who had tattoos, and no matter how hard he tried, he was unlikely to change those preconceptions in his lifetime. Next time he went for an interview he wore a long-sleeved shirt—and that time got the job.

CREATING A STRATEGY

How do you plan your marketing strategy? A starting point is to write down all your personal characteristics in two columns, one of them strengths and the other weaknesses.

Look at the list of weaknesses. Can you change them? Or eliminate them altogether? Now look at your list of strengths. Can you promote them in either a business or a personal sense?

Approaching the task methodically like this helps you keep a clear idea of what you're trying to do. It's not an ego-driven self-promotion but a necessary career function, like compiling a CV.

A second step towards successfully marketing yourself is to get rid of the employee mindset. By regarding yourself not as an employee but as a one-person business, you can effect a significant change in your life. If you're a receptionist, see yourself as Me Inc, a business that's been hired by the company to do a magnificent job greeting customers and answering phones. Even when I was earning $60 a week as a junior in a real estate office, I imagined myself to be the boss of my own company. It was only a vision, but it did produce an important shift in attitude which affected the way I did the job. If you act *as if* you own the business, you'll be more committed to what you're doing.

Don't imagine that you need public relations flair to market yourself. All you need is a sensible strategy. I was anything but a born public speaker. In an earlier chapter I told the story of how I forced myself to do a Toastmasters course. My objective then was to prepare myself for work in sales. A few years later, when I'd started to make some headway in the real estate business, I was invited to the Real Estate Institute to speak to other agents on selling methods. I wasn't paid to do it and only about ten agents turned up to listen, but I enjoyed the experience and it gave me the idea of using public speaking as a means of networking.

The idea grew from there and today making speeches is an important part of my personal marketing strategy. I enjoy it, I get well paid for it and there are various spin-offs for my business. Each year I speak to about 10 000 people around Australia plus a large number of people overseas. Each time I get up to speak I have two objectives. Firstly, I hope to provide the audience with information and inspiration. Secondly, I'm hoping they will get to know me and that this will ultimately help my business. In other words, by telling the story of how our business operates, I'm simultaneously promoting it.

RELIABILITY COUNTS

What personal qualities do people respond to most? I said before that honesty was the most important of all. Reliability is another. You must do whatever you promise to do: anyone who doesn't will find it hard to survive long in the commercial world.

The willingness to go the extra mile is another positive quality. Don't just do what's expected of you but do a little bit more. Walt Disney called it 'delivering plus one per cent'. Whatever line of business you're in, you can always find a way to do it a little bit better. That's what keeps me interested after nearly twenty years in real estate.

People also respond well to confidence. If you're confident in yourself, others feel confident in you. How do you acquire confidence? The best way is to become an expert at what you're doing. In selling, this means acquiring product knowledge. Most people acquire enough product knowledge to get by. But I suggest you acquire so much knowledge that everyone in the market wants to deal with you. Not just customers, either. When you make yourself an expert, you'll find that other staff and even your boss will start coming to you to make use of your knowledge. When I was about twenty, I knew I was on the right track when others in the office, including some who'd been in the business for ten years or more, started coming to me and asking me questions about technical information because I'd taken the time to learn about it.

It doesn't matter if you're selling real estate, or working in a florist's shop or driving a bus: you can make yourself the best informed at what you do. If you do this, it will certainly be noticed, and inevitably it will benefit your career. You're sure to get ahead. Try it and see if I'm right.

The habit of making money

Wealth is not a mystery. While there's no magic formula for it, you can change your mind-set to attract wealth to you overnight.

You may need to first rid yourself of the belief that you're somehow not the 'wealth-creating type'. Okay, so you came from a working-class family. That doesn't mean you have to stay that way. Many people live a few thousand dollars in the red year after year and accept this as their lot. They cannot imagine themselves living any other way. What you need to do is replace this limiting belief with a belief that, no matter who you are or what you do, it's within your power to build wealth.

But what's the big deal about money? After all,

it's just zeros in a bankbook. The answer might seem obvious, but the question's still worth asking. Financial security should be your first objective. Sure, it's nice to build your wealth and be able to reward yourself for your diligence with nice things, but the dollars themselves are not the real reward. It's the peace of mind that comes with taking control of your life and not having the constant concern of how you'll pay next week's rent.

There are so many people I know who are constantly one pay cheque away from disaster—forever borrowing from people to pay others they already owe money to. They're waiting on next week's salary cheque to pay last month's mortgage or rent. It becomes a vicious circle, and living like this creates feelings of instability, uncertainty and fear, all of which inhibit your ability to achieve success in other key areas of your life. The good news is that this 'old state' can be overridden within a short period.

Ask most people what the main cause of stress and worry in their life is, and you'll often find it's a financial problem of some kind. If you can rid yourself of this one big problem by sensible saving and budgeting, your life will take on a new flavour.

Suddenly, you'll be able to enjoy the freedom that comes from not having to worry about whether you can pay for your next purchase. Without that stress, your health will improve, and you will certainly be in a better position to achieve business and personal goals. It's when you feel financially secure and confident that you're best able to go out and perform.

The people I know who have managed to achieve financial success have one thing in common: they're not afraid of money. In this respect, they differ from most other people. Most people think that money is hard to get and hard to keep; they worry that it might get them into trouble (remember the saying 'money is the root of all evil'?). By contrast, people who make a lot of money see money merely as a tool, a commodity. They're not intimidated by it. They feel comfortable and confident dealing with it.

You hear some people say that they're 'bad with money'. What this actually means is that they make bad money decisions day to day. You also hear it said that people are 'good with money'. The idea is that the people who make money have a natural flair for it. This isn't true either. I was hopeless when it came to money in my early years. I was bad at maths, I never studied economics and I had no interest in financial matters generally. I also had an 'anti-money' mind-set. These days I consider myself a successful money manager, but everything I know about the subject had to be learned.

So, nobody is inherently bad with money. It's just that some people are disciplined with money—they budget, save and invest—and others aren't disciplined. The undisciplined group get their pay cheque each week and spend until it's gone.

Why? One reason is that many people create a financial facade for themselves: they try to maintain a lifestyle of affluence that they struggle to afford. For instance, you often find young people renting accommodation that is well beyond their budget. They're trying to create an image of success to impress their peers.

The solution is simple: live within your means. If all you can afford is a small apartment at $130 a week, that's what you should be living in right now. If people think the worse of you for that, that's their problem!

In my early days in real estate a salesman a few years older than me used to rent an incredibly expensive apartment. In today's dollars, it might have cost him $1500 a week, which is a lot for a single guy. To this day, he still doesn't own any real estate of his own. He spent all his money maintaining a lifestyle that he couldn't afford and had none left to invest. So, live within your means and budget.

The need to create an external image to make others feel better about you can be a financial trap in a number of ways. To avoid it, you need to be comfortable with who you are. You shouldn't be dependant on recognition from others. You ought to be able to say, that's the place I can afford to live, that's the car I can afford to drive, that's the holiday I can afford to go on, that's the restaurant where I can afford to eat.

CONTROLLING YOUR OUTGOINGS

When I left school I learned the hard way to live within my means. At the time I'd been out of work for eight weeks, but I was still spending with a credit card that one of the banks had been foolish enough to give me. One day I went into a shop to buy a gift for my girlfriend. I handed over the credit card for payment, and the shop assistant phoned the bank to check my credit level. While this was happening I stood at the counter with my heart pounding. I feared the card was over the limit and I was terrified it would be handed back to me and I'd be refused the purchase. What happened was far worse. The shop assistant hung up the phone, picked up a pair of scissors and cut up the card in front of me, explaining that the bank had asked her to destroy it. I felt sick with embarrassment. It remains one of the most uncomfortable memories of my life.

This awful incident did teach me a lesson, though. After that I resolved to become more responsible. My first job in real estate earned me $60 a week, which wasn't much even back then. At first I used to put the $60 straight in my wallet and spend it as the need arose. With the credit-card incident still fresh in my memory, I quickly recognised that unless I took control of my money I would again end up in financial trouble. So I took five envelopes, and with a black marker pen I wrote on them Food, Rent, Clothing, Entertainment and Savings.

When I was paid each week I'd go back to my flat and distribute the $60 in the envelopes. Whenever

I needed money during the following week I'd take it from the appropriate envelope—but never from another envelope. It was a crude budgeting system, but it did stop me overspending and being unable to pay for essentials. Ever since then I have continued to manage my financial affairs in a similar way. The system I use now might be a bit more sophisticated and computerised, but the underlying principle is the same.

Failure to keep outgoings under tight control can be a problem in business, too. I was guilty of it myself once. I used to think that sales equalled success. In other words, I didn't realise the difference between revenue and profit and I knew nothing about cash flow. I remember going to a real estate conference in San Francisco and being phoned by my accountant, who said, 'You'd better come home. We've got no money in the account to pay the wages.' What had happened was that I had delegated the job of signing cheques to someone else in the organisation, and he was signing cheques as fast as he could put pen to paper. In effect, I had surrendered control of a vital activity in the company's operation without regard to the consequences.

So I had to come home to deal with the crisis. From that day on, I have kept an extremely tight control on costs. Every month I go through our accounts in detail, querying even the smallest expenditure if I think this is warranted. After all, small costs, if there are enough of them, add up to big costs.

I learned my lesson in this from Ted Wright, who ran the Regent Hotel in Sydney for many years and was regarded as one of the country's outstanding hotel operators. Ted used to sign every cheque paid by the Regent, regardless of whether the cheque was for $50 or $500 000. That impressed me, as I knew the Regent was an extremely large and well-run operation. Here was the Chief Executive with a lot on his plate who still considered it an essential part of his role to know every cost incurred by his organisation. I decided this was a great example to follow. Previously, I'd felt I was too busy to be signing cheques.

To take firm control of your outgoings, the most effective way is to have a personal budget and stick to it. To open a business without a budget would be regarded as financial insanity. But it's just as crazy not to have a personal budget. Note that your budget shouldn't just be for the coming week; it should take account of what you will need to spend in the next twelve months. If you intend going on a holiday later in the year, you'll need to start setting aside money for it now. It should be factored into your budget.

MAXIMISING YOUR INCOME

So far I've spoken about controlling your outgoings. The other key to saving is, of course, maximising your income. Obviously, you need to work at both ends: maximising what you earn and controlling what you spend.

How you go about maximising what you earn will naturally depend on your own circumstances. When I was about 20, I tried to do this by working at multiple jobs. I did a newspaper run early in the morning, spent the day working at the real estate office, cleaned the office after work for extra money and finally worked at a hotel collecting glasses. This increased my income, but after six months I felt burnt out. I was working from 5.00 a.m. to midnight, then crawling into bed only to be awoken, what seemed like minutes later by the alarm. I made the decision that the best way to earn more money was to become really expert at one thing. For me, this was to be selling real estate. I have been intensely focused now on real estate for almost twenty years. The decision turned out to be the right one.

If you increase significantly the value of what you contribute—if you increase significantly the quality of your work, your product knowledge, your skills, your capability—your income will increase significantly too.

This requires you to make a leap of faith, knowing there'll be a lag time between the extra effort you inject and the financial rewards you'll pick up down the track. Let's say you're an administrative assistant earning $30 000 a year in an office. You might be surrounded by other employees earning commissions and bonuses and therefore making a lot more money than you are. Unfair? Possibly not. That may well be an accurate measure of what you're contributing—$30 000 of value each year to that business. So what can you do if you want to get ahead?

You can make the leap of faith and massively

increase your contribution. Improve the accuracy of your work; improve your typing speed; try to contribute elsewhere—look for opportunities to add value to other areas of the business, whether you're paid for it or not. Sooner or later the extra contribution will be recognised and translate into additional income. It's guaranteed.

This was my own approach when I started in real estate. I was absolutely confident that if I kept adding value at a higher rate consistently and reliably, it would pay off. I worked longer hours than other people in the office. I used to work on Sunday showing people rental accommodation, even though I was on a fixed wage and not earning any commission. Others in the office thought I was crazy. But it paid off. What it did was sculpt work attitudes and work habits that I took to the next job I had, then to the job after that, and finally to my own business. In effect, I was training myself—developing a can-do, go-the-extra-mile, do-what-it-takes, it's-my-pleasure attitude. It took three years but it eventually paid off.

By all means take on an extra job or two to earn extra money in the short term. But I found it isn't the best long-term wealth-creation strategy. Much better to choose one thing that you excel at (or have the potential to excel at) and you feel passionate about, then set out to become the best. Work at your job as a craft with the intention of becoming the best at it in the world. Before long, the effort will pay off tenfold.

CONTROLLING YOUR DESTINY

Money assists us to take control of our lives—it is certainly not the end goal, in my opinion. Once you have achieved a certain level of financial security and have an investment and wealth-creation plan, the rest is somewhat academic. Whether you end up with $1 million or $10 million is far less important than achieving a sense of control over your destiny. Remember that we all need only a limited amount of money to enjoy a perfectly comfortable lifestyle. We can drive only one car, sleep in one bed, wear one outfit and visit one holiday destination at a time. The old saying that the best things in life are free is very true.

If, as you read this, you're suffering pain financially, it may not be such a bad thing in the overall picture. Take advantage of the pain: use it to strengthen your resolve to take control of this area of your life. Decide from now on to act responsibly where money is concerned.

Let's say you're $10 000 in the red and feeling overwhelmed by it. You can't see any way out. You must readjust your thinking to know that there *is* a way. I'm not saying you will fix the problem overnight. You probably won't get out of debt and acquire a $1 million portfolio of shares in twelve months, but you can, most likely, pay off your $10 000 debt in two years. Provided you have a positive mindset about it. And provided you believe that it's definitely within your power to transform your financial situation.

INVESTING IN WEALTH

In the last few pages we looked at the vital importance of living within your means by keeping within a budget. Now we come to the second rule of wealth creation. That is: invest your excess income in capital-appreciating assets.

Let's say you're earning $500 a week after tax and spending $450. What do you do with the $50 you have over? It's an important question. Some people would say: 'Why bother saving and investing such a small amount of money? There's surely no point.' Why not start saving and investing when you get further along in your career and start earning more money?

This is how people begin a lifelong habit of not saving and investing. They wait for a day of excess income that never arrives. The time to start your saving and investing habit is today. This is what investing should become—a habit. As a matter of course, week after week, you should keep putting excess money into capital-appreciating assets. If the money you have to spare at the end of each week is only $50, that's okay. Investing $50 each week is a great start. The law of accumulation says that $50 invested each week will amount to thousands and thousands of dollars in a few years.

So, what should you invest in? My personal view

is there are two sensible possibilities: property and shares. There are plenty of other ways you can invest your money, of course, but unless you're an expert investor most are potentially risky. Personally, I'm a conservative money manager—an investor rather than a speculator. Speculating in high-risk shares is certainly an option, but it's not one I recommend. Blue-chip shares are a more sensible choice. Unless you're a skilled operator, the top 100 stocks are probably the best place to put your money.

It's the same with buying property. Unless you're an expert, you'd be wise to avoid speculative developments. Buy in areas that have a track record for growth and rental income. And buy something you're familiar and comfortable with. Some people buy property interstate or overseas. My advice is, don't buy a property that you can't drive past whenever you want to. If the property's near enough to drive past, it will be a lot easier to monitor and manage and you'll be far more likely to make the right investment decision in the first place.

I said before that people who have made a lot of money typically have no fear of money. In my experience, they have another thing in common: they do their homework before they go into an investment. Nothing is done on a whim, or left to chance. If it's the stock market they intend to invest in, or if it's the property market, they make a close study of it beforehand, and they know precisely what return they're getting or likely to get.

I have found that most investors have only a vague idea about this. It's rare for owners of rental properties to know what their percentage return is. If you ask them, they usually reply, 'I'm not exactly sure.' Obviously, it's not something they consider important. Yet if people do not know what their return is, they cannot possibly judge if the investment is a good or bad one and, therefore, whether they should be building on the investment or pulling out.

Don't hesitate to obtain professional advice before investing your money. What you stand to gain is well worth the adviser's fee. No matter how much research we do, we can't become experts at everything ourselves, so it makes sense to consult someone who is an expert. Kerry Packer, Rupert Murdoch and all the other successful people I know in the business world consult experts, so why not us?

EXERCISE PATIENCE

Obviously, some patience is required if you want to be a successful investor. If you expect to become wealthy in a matter of months, you're likely to be disappointed. Most people overestimate how much money they can save and invest in the first year. On the other hand, most people underestimate how much money they can accumulate in five years.

When I first began selling, my boss suggested to me that I should live off my wage and save my commissions. It was good advice. My wage was a modest base salary, but it was enough to get by on. So each time I received a commission cheque I'd go to the bank and deposit it in an investment account that I'd opened specially for this purpose. I'd put the money in each week and forget about it. I deliberately avoided checking on the balance. When eventually I did check, I found there was $20 000 there, which was enough for me to put down a deposit on a property. I borrowed the rest and this was my first purchase of real estate.

For most of us, borrowing is an unfortunate necessity when buying a property. We have to do it, but we ought to keep it to a minimum. There is a simple principle to follow: borrow as little as you need to advance yourself financially. If you can make the purchase by borrowing 70 per cent instead of 80 per cent of the price, borrow the 70 per cent.

MILLIONARES FOR A MOMENT

Recently a survey was done of people in the United States who'd had lottery wins of over a million dollars. It was found that within a few years of winning the money, a large proportion of the people were worse off financially than they had been in the first place. On the face of it this seemed impossible: how could you win a million dollars or more and end up worse off? The explanation was that these people had never learned how to manage money. If they'd had to earn the money themselves, they would have learned this through experience. They would have learned the art of tending their investments like a garden, feeding and watering them every day and weeding out those that weren't doing well. Instead, by winning a suitcase of cash they developed extravagant spending habits which they'd never had before, yet they did not know how to save, retain and build on their winnings.

The truth is that very few of us get rich quickly. A handful of people try it and succeed, but most come unstuck. I once read of a young man who came into a large amount of money and used it to buy a nightclub. He said in an interview that he did it because it seemed a cool thing at the time and because he thought it would be a good way to meet girls. The point of the story was that he went broke and lost the lot in a few years. Quite apart from the dubious reasons he had for choosing this particular investment, his big mistake was that he got into something he knew nothing about. It's a common error.

I have a friend I grew up with who for the whole of his working life has been looking for a get-rich scheme. As I write this, he's now in his mid-thirties and he still hasn't found one. I took the other, tortoise-like approach: conservatively building up assets bit by bit. He's looking for the big hit and I hope one day he finds it. The trouble is: I'm not sure there are many big hits to be found, and a lot of people go broke looking for them. When it comes to investing your hard-earned money, it's much wiser to have a measured, strategic approach.

Learning: **Creating wealth is a skill that can be learned like playing a musical instrument or a new sport. Figure out the rules, develop the necessary skills and implement a wealth plan today.**

Some final tips for success and growth

WHETHER YOU THINK YOU CAN OR YOU CAN'T; YOU'RE RIGHT!

This quote from the great Henry Ford really sums up the critical importance of optimistic and positive thought. If you truly believe in something, it's 75 per cent achieved already. Whatever anyone has ever done on this marvellous planet is available to you also. It's not a question of 'whether', it's only a question of 'how?'.

BE PASSIONATE

Be passionate about whatever you do. Life is an incredible journey and every day a new adventure unfolds. Get excited about everything you're involved in. When you get excited it's infectious and those around will want to be part of your vision.

THINK BIGGER

There are many examples of miracles all around us. Whatever you can think of, or dream of, do it. There are no limits upon possibility other than those you place upon yourself. Be daring and reach for the highest stars. We were all created to be great. Any variation from this greatness is of our own choosing.

BE FOCUSED

Determine your path in life and create a plan or road map for greatness. Once you have set your course, develop laser-beam focus and let nothing distract you from your life purpose. There will always be a myriad of events sent to take your attention off the main game. See these as opportunities to strengthen your resolve.

LOOK AFTER OTHERS

We are all part of the same extended family. Look after those around you, whether you know them well or not. A starving child in Africa is a problem for all of us, not just some of us. Nurture people; encourage them to be the best they can be. Every one of us has greatness within.

WHEN THE DREAM IS BIG ENOUGH THE ODDS DON'T MATTER

Dream of the life you want for yourself and your loved ones. It will appear, given time to cultivate the necessary elements. And life will throw you challenges consistently. See them as a gift. They can all teach you valuable lessons and none can stop you from achieving your own greatness—from living your dream. Persist until it happens, for if you persist, it will.

Before you go

So now you're in the home straight—you've all but finished the book. I'm hopeful that already you've had some insight into the simple secrets of success, or maybe even implemented successfully some new life strategies. This is, in essence, why I wrote the book. To be a catalyst—to stir something up in your heart to get you to take action in the direction of your dreams. To remind you that you do have control over your destiny and that you are the keeper of the keys to that magic kingdom called a magnificent life.

If we open our eyes we can see there's a world around us that is full of inspiration. What we need to do is look for the inspiration every day, whether in books, tapes, on television or the Internet, or maybe in someone sitting next to you. Almost everything around you has the potential to inspire you if you're seeking inspiration. So look for it everywhere. Then, suddenly, you'll find that the world is really a place full of opportunities.

One quick word of warning: beware the Dream Takers. There are many people who have not yet developed an abundance mentality. That is, they don't yet understand that by supporting and encouraging you to succeed it can become a springboard for their own successes—if they cheer you on from the sidelines if you like. In fact, some people feel inadequate in the face of others moving to new levels of performance. So don't let the Dream Takers spoil your journey. Accept that some people will cheer you on and others will not.

It's an exciting time to be alive. We have never had as many opportunities as we do today: opportunities to learn, to travel, to experience new things, to create new enterprises. This is a time to excel. We can do things today that we couldn't have dreamt of doing a few years ago.

Often you hear people talk about the 'halcyon

days—the good old days'. Well, right now we're living in the good old days. In 20 or 30 years' time, people will look back on the period we're living in and see these as the halcyon years. Don't wait until then to recognise this for the truly exciting time that it is. Recognise it now. Don't end up down the track wishing you could turn back the clock. Make the decisions today that will provide you with the results you deserve.

The present and future is what's important, not the past. If until now you've felt you've had an average or even disappointing life, realise that that your old life can end right now. Too many people allow the failures of the past to pollute their future.

As you arrive at this last page of the book, my hope is that your life will have changed. If what you've just read has been of value to you, make sure you hold on to it and do something with it. Make new decisions. Create a new attitude. Develop a new mind-set. Your future is a blank canvas on which you can create your every dream. Do it with excitement, courage and passion.

Travel safely on your journey and I hope that our paths may cross.